I'd Rather Do
CHEMO

Than Clean Out the Garage

I'd Rather Do CHEMO

Than Clean Out the Garage

Choosing Laughter over Tears

FRAN DI GIACOMO

Illustrations by Marc Di Giacomo

BROWN BOOKS PUBLISHING GROUP
DALLAS, TEXAS

For information, please contact
Brown Books Publishing Group
16200 North Dallas Parkway, Suite 170
Dallas, Texas 75248
www.brownbooks.com
972-381-0009

ISBN 0-9713265-2-5
LCCN 2003096174

First Printing, 2003
Second Printing, 2004

Thank you to these stars in my crown:

★

My sister, Marilyn, who is my best friend

★

My beautiful sons, Marc and Eric, who always make me proud

★

Most importantly, to my wonderful husband, Len,
who is my editor-in-residence,
my knight on a white horse,
my precious treasure,
the wind beneath my wings,
who supports me in everything I do,
and gives me the freedom to fail.

Contents

Foreword

*C*ancer. *The "Big C."* It is never expected, never wished for, and never welcomed. It is often met with disbelief, anger, and the instinctual response of, *"Why ME?"* The diagnosis of cancer will forever change a person's life. It will also forever change the lives of that person's family, friends, and loved ones. It is an unexpected detour on life's journey, but the road traveled doesn't have to be full of rocks or potholes (chuckholes for you in the South). Rather, it can lead to a remarkable adventure for those who want to learn how to experience it.

Battling cancer requires incredible courage, inner strength, humility, spirituality, and, quite often, a bit of humor. *I'd Rather Do Chemo Than Clean Out the Garage* is an incredible account of one woman's life with cancer. The vignettes are utterly hilarious and, although sometimes a little wicked, truly portray her character and perseverance, which are fed by the side-splitting humor that can be extracted from many of the daily drudgeries associated with cancer care. (WARNING: DO NOT READ THIS BOOK IN THE IMMEDIATE POSTOPERATIVE PERIOD FOR RISK OF POPPING A SUTURE OR STAPLE CLOSURE.) From dealing with wigs gone awry to making the best of each hospitalization, the skills of finding positive aspects in one of life's most frightful changes are conveyed with humor in this book.

Anyone experiencing cancer will embrace these lighthearted depictions of the struggle to survive and will recognize the powerful, positive impact of the human spirit. After all, you can choose to cry—or you can choose to laugh until you cry.

You may ask if I am truly qualified to write this foreword. Have I had cancer? No. However, I have learned how to attain strength and courage through humor from the remarkable woman who is the author of this book. I have traveled the road with her as I have with many other women battling gynecologic cancers. The lessons learned from their journeys have enriched my life, and I hope this book will impact your personal battle or your loved one's battle with cancer. Laughter truly is good medicine.

Carolyn Y. Muller, MD
Gynecologic Oncology
UT Southwestern Medical Center, Dallas, Texas

Preface

L ife was good for our family. My husband's business was growing, our oldest son decided he was grown up enough to spend two whole weeks at summer camp, and our youngest son discovered baseball. Then I discovered a lump in my breast—not surprising since my mother died of cancer at forty-six and my brother at forty-two. I was forty years old and carrying on the family tradition. Suddenly, surgery and chemotherapy consumed our lives.

Despite having vigilant checkups at every prescribed interval, a second cancer appeared with a vengeance when I was fifty-four: wildly out-of-control ovarian cancer. How did this happen under a doctor's care? (That story is another book.) This time the surgery was mentally, physically, and emotionally devastating.

Bombed out from the chemo and pain medication, I moved like a zombie from bed to sofa to recliner and back to bed. My brain drifted in and out of the fog. If you've been through this, you know the routine. Whenever the mental mists lifted, I'd reach for one of the dozens of books brought by caring and concerned friends.

One by one I took a book from the top of the stack, searching for inspiration and wisdom. One by one, I rejected them all. They were too meditative, somber, or sentimental. They made me cry, since they all seemed devoted to helping me learn to die. An ancient emperor of Rome said, "How shameful and absurd it is for the spirit to surrender when the body is able to fight on." Well, it was pretty clear at this point that my body wasn't doing its fair share, so my spirit was going to have to take up the slack! I decided not to live my life planning to die.

Do I have to tell you how many copies of the famous "chicken soup" series found their way to the mountain of books by my chair?

I picked up the first copy and dutifully began reading. Within minutes I was learning about someone who, when diagnosed with cancer, spent the next several months in a mindless stupor, not even communicating with his family. And one day—hello!—realizing that he was not dead yet, got up and had dinner with his wife and children (that's basically the story—honest).

In disgust, I heaved the book across the room. *Out of my sight, you purveyor of doom and gloom!* I thought, before picking up yet another "soup." Chapter after chapter the sob stories dribbled, creating a large puddle in my lap.

Oh, wait. That's just my IV leaking.

Okay, so the book wasn't leaking on my lap. But it did make that airborne leap across the room where all the other rejects lay in a jumbled heap.

Bored and more than just a little frustrated, I reached for one more book and began reading. It turned out to be hysterically funny!

Then I realized that laughing energized me—so laughter and the energy it produced quickly became my weapon against infirmity. Let me explain.

At the time of diagnosis I was, and still am, a professional artist. Galleries in several states represent my still life and landscape paintings. My oil portraits include families, sports figures, and dignitaries. Over three million prints of my artworks have been sold. In the last five years I was hospitalized thirteen times, had nine additional surgeries, entered two more galleries, earned signature status in one of the most prominent art organizations in the United States, produced three one-woman exhibits, painted numerous exciting portraits, and was published in *Who's Who of American Women* and *Who's Who in American Art*— all while on continuous chemotherapy.

How? Laughter helped me do it.

Why did I write this book? For my own amusement and hopefully yours.

Acknowledgments

❧

To Carolyn Muller, MD, FACOG (Isn't that impressive?)
University of Texas Southwestern Medical Center, Dallas, Texas
who keeps me alive and kicking.

❧

To Christian Renna, DO
Lifespan Medicine, Dallas, Texas
who keeps me healthy.

❧

To Marlane Miller for her super-cosmic support
and for her book,
Brainstyles™: Change Your Life Without Changing Who You Are
I strongly urge you to read this book.
Have a friend pick it up at the bookstore.

❧

To Jean Hoffman for *101 lunches*
and for being my personal typist and word processor.

I was reeling from the effects of chemo and pain
medication, when I reached into the mountain of
books, picked a humorous one, and began to read.

chapter 1

Laughter Really Is the Best Medicine

SURVIVAL SECRET ONE

Laughter Will Set You Free!

This is it, folks. I am drawing the line in the sand to separate the *haves* from the *have-nots,* the *wishers* from the *want-nots,* the *doers* from the *do-nots.*

If you are the weepy, whiny, noodle-spined sort who loves to drown in those "soupy" books, I invite you to try it my way. If you prefer to weep and wail, dissolving into fits of self-pity, I *implore* you to try it my way. Like the sirens in Homer beckoning you to forbidden and unfamiliar shores, I beg you: *give laughter a chance.*

In my seventeen years as a flight attendant (oh, that was before I was a successful artist), I was able to observe human nature—a lot! One thing became very clear. Some people possess an unusual penchant for drama and trauma. They aren't happy unless they are miserable. For these folks a calm life needs a monkey wrench to set off more turbulence. I guess this is what you call "thriving on chaos." The only thing that makes them feel better is more tears—and more chaos. Okay, before you think I have no feelings, you need to know that I respect the fact that sometimes you need a good cry to get the dust out of your eyes. But do we have to *stay* there? Not me. Maybe not you either.

Have I cried? Absolutely. Will I cry again? Undeniably. Do I occasionally get despondent? Unquestionably. But quite frankly, I just don't *enjoy* it! Misery takes a great deal of energy and makes me feel bad. As I see my path becoming shorter and narrower I have to ask myself, "How do I want to spend my time?"

The answer always comes back: laughing out loud. I want to spend my time laughing! Why have I developed all kinds of devious and carefully orchestrated methods to achieve laughter? Because it makes me feel good. I need to feel good! (I'll bet you do too.)

Wait a minute. I hear you asking some obvious questions. *What about God? Doesn't she seek solace in her Creator?* Absolutely, yes. *Then why is laughter her strength?* My answer is this: I know God exists. I thank Him daily for my ability to create beautiful art and the brains to do it. I know that the power of prayer has kept me going for years against insurmountable odds. I also know that our Creator has an incredible sense of humor. You only have to observe nature for an instant to recognize this. And I know that He has empowered all of us with the gift of mirth and the strength to laugh. But it's up to us to use it. So if you realize that laughter is one of God's great gifts, then you know you're supposed to laugh. It's the eleventh commandment. *Thou shalt laugh.*

So give me the warped, wicked, fun-loving, wretched yearning to breathe free! Let's pull up those gut-wrenching, incision-splitting belly laughs that are hidden somewhere among the tumors, blood clots, and dark recesses of our souls. All of us have been given the healing and restorative gift of mirth, but I dare to speculate that some of you have probably been ignoring yours.

Remember: where there is humor there is hope.

It's just that simple. A sick mind cannot help a sick body. Laughter frees the mind from the shackles of despair and, in turn, empowers the body. This is neither chemo voodoo nor pseudo psychobabble. I know firsthand that when you ride the cancer roller coaster, you are so frantically clutching the handlebars and wild-eyed with terror that you forget to enjoy the dizzying heights.

Understandably, you have probably failed to see the beauty and humor around you. As a result, you tend to ignore the *benefits* of the chemo lifestyle! If you have your doubts, you're just going to have to trust me on this one.

Laughter is a great healer, as I discovered quite by accident. A little background:

I went to the oncologist for my annual cancer checkup and was relieved to learn that things were fine. About a month later, however, I had a pain in my abdomen. I went back to the doctor (who has since been condemned to Dante's Inferno) for more tests. Suspecting the worst, I asked for and received full-body CT scans and a battery of other tests. The nurse called me the next day to come review the results.

When I woke up that morning, I somehow knew in my soul that my life would never be the same again. I had a tennis game with friends scheduled before the doctor's appointment, and I figured I might as well go since *I may never get to play tennis again*. Besides, why ruin my whole day? After the match, as we were chatting over glasses of iced tea, I told my friends what I suspected. My own personal form of group therapy had begun.

As it turns out, I was diagnosed with ovarian cancer stage IIIC—not good. I went home from the doctor's office filled with dread about telling my husband that cancer had returned to our lives. His life, too, was going to be changed forever.

He came home for dinner and we stood in the kitchen trading stories about the day's events. Finally I told him the news. We looked at each other for a long time, letting it all sink in. He broke the silence by saying softly, "I know we're supposed to go to that party tonight, but I think we need to stay home."

"No!" I stated so emphatically that it even took me by surprise. "If ever there was a time when we need to go out and enjoy a glass of wine and laugh with friends, it's now. I refuse to stay home and wallow in self-pity."

"Are you sure?" he asked incredulously.

"Positive!" I replied, my personal survival strategy already taking shape.

A few days later I was sent off to surgery, where they removed massive multiple blobs and globs from my abdominal cavity. While they were in there, they also took out various other parts, particles, and anything else they could get to turn loose.

After seven hours, the surgeon was growing weary of his seek-and-destroy mission and stapled me shut. They took out so much that I still rattle when I walk.

The recovery was war. For some reason, all my remaining guts forgot what they were there for and refused to function. My body didn't know how to accept, digest, process, or eliminate food. Hey, I'm not whining. Those are simply the facts and I include them so you will know from whence I come. But I also promise you will never hear me complain like *that* again. It's not nearly creative enough. Whining that is both productive and creative, on the other hand, is an accomplished skill and one that you too can achieve as you benefit from my years of experience.

It was during this time, reeling from the effects of chemo and pain medication, that I searched the mountain of books and found that humor was the answer. Giggle was good, chuckle was better. Then I laughed—great gales of laughter. It felt so good. I had to clutch a pillow over my midsection to keep from ripping open my seams. But how wonderful it was! After thirty minutes, I was energized. I could get up and move around the house, attending to light tasks that I had been ignoring (such as putting food in my mouth). A few days of returning for repeated doses of laughter, and I realized I had enough energy to sit at the easel and paint—food for my soul. I didn't want it to stop.

When concerned friends asked what they could do, I said, "bring me anything funny."

Speaking of painting I must confess something, since no good book is worth its salt without at least one confession. None of the galleries across the country who carry my work has been aware of my medical problems. I have been living a double life. Art is my fantasy world, whereas my medical life is reality. Amazingly, I have been able to keep these two worlds from colliding. By writing this book, I am literally "coming out of the cancer closet."

Thanks to laughter, I've been able to keep the galleries supplied with paintings. By now you've got it: laughter gives me energy, a zest for life, and mental enthusiasm. All that mental enthusiasm can make up for a lot of body aches!

I maintain my double life by speaking with the galleries by phone when I'm upbeat and visiting them in person when I'm able to stand. Sometimes I feel like dog meat, but the outing does me immeasurable good. I even do painting demonstrations during special exhibits. Granted, sometimes it takes massive doses of over-the-counter painkillers and more than a small bit of mental and physical effort, but somehow the pieces fit together when supported with the power of laughter.

There have been times when it seemed overwhelming to keep my two worlds separate and independent. But I just kept putting one foot in front of the other. When I was still in the hospital after surgery, my husband came in one day and told me I'd received a phone call from a potential client who wanted a landscape five feet high and seven feet long. I love to paint landscapes, but when my bleary brain visualized such an enormous canvas, I moaned and pushed the morphine button. At that moment, I truly believed my "client" days were over. The future looked really bleak. I drifted off to sleep, convinced I could never do it.

In the days of recuperation at home, my mind kept wandering back to that painting. I hated to let it go. It would be so much fun. Still, I was almost sure it would be impossible. Common sense told me to forget it and just concentrate on smaller, more manageable canvases for the galleries. When I finally returned the client's phone call, the chemo was pounding away at me and my voice was so weak I could barely speak. I apologized for not returning his call earlier (I told him I'd been out of town) and asked him to excuse my "laryngitis." I figured there was no harm in at least finding out what he wanted. As I listened to him explain his requirements, I knew I really wanted to do this painting. Could I do it? I bought some time by making our initial appointment for three weeks later.

Anticipating the steady loss of my hair, I wore my wig for our first meeting in order to present a consistent hairstyle over the months it would take to finish this painting. When he arrived to review my portfolio and see some originals, I was still very weak and casually leaned against the wall for support as we looked at my paintings. He liked my work and we set another meeting for three weeks later at his house. I still couldn't drive, so my husband chauffeured. Over the next two months I bought more time between meetings.

Finally I was ready to order the canvas and begin the painting. Whenever the chemo was making mincemeat of my legs, I sat down and worked on the bottom portion of the canvas. When I could stand up, I painted the top half. The client was elated with the finished product, never suspecting that I started everyday with a dose of giggles and humor to get the energy to paint. My professional life became a continual pattern of laughter, willpower, and paint. I couldn't begin to tell you how many pieces of art have been squeezed in between surgeries and chemo. One Thanksgiving I received a request for a painting to be delivered by Christmas, a seasonal pattern in my business where panic management seems to rule. Because of prior obligations to other clients, there is usually no way I can fill these late requests.

This time it was possible. I could put aside the painting already in progress and try to meet the deadline. The challenge was that the chemotherapy I'd been receiving wasn't reducing the cancer, and my doctor had suggested we try another drug. We could only guess how my body would react, but history suggested I would wind up in the hospital. Still, the idea proposed by the client sounded like too much fun to miss. This large painting would be an action portrait of a well-known athlete and a Christmas present to be hung in a suite at the sports arena. My husband was sitting across the room from me when the call came in. When I hung up, he looked at me as though I had six heads.

"I can't believe you told her you could deliver that by Christmas!" he exclaimed.

In all honesty, I couldn't either. All I knew was I wanted to try. The painting was started on a Saturday morning. On Monday, I began the new chemo. On Wednesday—yep, sure enough—I was hospitalized with a severe allergic reaction. But by the following weekend, I was back in my studio and working on the painting. There was no time to waste, and I only had two weeks to finish it before my next chemo cycle. Confident I could pull it off, I made an appointment for my client to view the finished product.

The viewing went extremely well and the painting was approved. I was in the homestretch, and I had three weeks to let the painting dry before putting on the final glaze. I set a "cast-in-concrete" date for the finished art to be picked up. Actually, it had to be picked up then because I was going back to the hospital the next day. Again, the client never knew.

How did I finish the painting on time? Every minute I was receiving chemo infusion or was in the hospital, I was mentally painting that portrait. I was so excited about the painting that I filled the long, difficult days by making every brush stroke in my head. When I finally got to my studio, all of the decisions had been made, all the problems solved, and the paint flowed with rapid-fire execution.

Why am I boring you with these details? Because I know too many of you out there in the Chemo Club have given up and let the cancer treatment run (and ruin) your lives. I'll admit to doing the same thing in the very beginning. But in my five years on chemo, I have used laughter and mental enthusiasm to conquer giants. For example, I frequently have to make personal appearances at galleries for special exhibits of my work. These events are set many months in advance. Who knows what my condition will be when the date finally arrives? I just know I'll stand up straight and try not to stumble or stammer. The chemo always seems to be grinding me into sausage patties. But I put on a happy face, and you know what? I always have a good time! The compliments from admiring collectors have me soaring on wings. You can't replace that kind of therapy.

What does this all mean? **FIND YOUR PASSION!** Find something you love that is stronger than cancer and focus on it—laughter will give you energy to get there.

I know it's still only the first chapter, but I want to tell you about . . .

SURVIVAL SECRET TWO

Friends

When I first started down the treatment trail and the chemo was hammering me, my husband was reluctant to make dinner plans with friends. When we did get together with friends, however, we quickly learned the enormous benefits. We laugh, we joke, and we have a great time. Understandably, my friends always express concern over my latest (or next) surgery, but we never dwell on it. Who would want to be around me if I was always down in the dumps and moaning endlessly about all the gory details? My friends are quite aware that I'm fighting an uphill battle. Enough said. We're there to have fun.

What's really interesting is that we've made a lot of new friends in the past few years—people we always wanted to get together with but could never find the time. Well, now we *make* the time. If I'm completely under the covers, that's one thing. But a few days later, I'll drag myself out. Just because my head is swimming, my body feels like it was run over by a semi, and my legs don't work is no excuse to stay home bored and wallowing in self-pity.

Sometimes when getting dressed, I look in the mirror and think, *I'll never get through this!* But as soon as we get together with friends and start swapping laughs and conversation, my head clears and we have a good time. I may collapse in bed as soon as we get home, but these outings are good for me and they certainly keep depression at bay.

Actually, I've become quite comfortable with the chemo lifestyle. It's not something I would have chosen of course. But as long as I'm here, I might as well enjoy the perks. Perks? Did I say *perks?* Yes, I did. I've actually become rather spoiled by chemo. Interested? Read on and explore this with me.

I have learned many creative ways to negotiate the roadblocks and rough waters of the chemo lifestyle.

chapter 2

Milking It for All It's Worth

Call me crazy (and most people do), but there really are a lot of benefits to a chemo lifestyle. As a career member of the Chemo Club, I have learned many creative ways to negotiate the roadblocks and rough waters of the chemo lifestyle. Let's examine the upside to all of this!

The Great Gift Caper

You may declare me a shameless hussy and accuse me of abusing my friends, but not to worry. I love my friends and do everything I can to take care of them.

You see, I've always been an independent person and not necessarily the touchy-feely type. But when my ship went down, I was amazed at how many people came to my rescue. At one point, I remarked to a friend that everyone should get hit by a truck just once to see how many people cared. Friends assigned themselves the task of bringing food to my family on a regular basis. Of course I thanked them profusely. But when the food had filled the freezer to overflowing and was beginning to pile up under the bushes behind my house, the meals-on-wheels people were soon stalking my house for leftovers. Still the food kept coming. Even now after five years, I come home and find goodies on my doorstep. Last Christmas there was a mountain of presents at my door. It was embarrassing. Imagine what that last person thought as they left their package on top of the pile.

Actually, I know what they thought: *Fran is milking this for all it's worth. Fran has learned the art of creative whining—just enough to keep the care packages coming but not enough to drive people away.*

Embarrassing, but true. One friend in particular brings me gifts constantly. Wonderful things. Little, thoughtful things. Frivolous things I would never buy for myself: lotions and potions for my body, snugly blankets, and an endless supply of chocolates. Oh, how I do love chocolate! (Did you hear about the guy who asked the genie to make him irresistible to women and the genie "zapped" him into a box of chocolates?) This friend also brings my other vital necessity: laughs. She has provided me with a lifetime supply of comedy tapes and funny jokes for "horizontal" days.

She still asks what she can bring to brighten my day. I was thinking of putting in a request for a new clothes dryer or dishwasher. Now that would really bolster my spirits! Then next (in a pitifully rasping voice), I could drop a "hint" that the disposal in my kitchen quit working years ago. And well, you know how it is with the new chemo and all . . . .

All of this attention is quite overwhelming! How do I show my appreciation? I truly don't have the energy level to get out and shop, and so I find it difficult to reciprocate. How can I express to this dear friend how much her support means to me? I'll have to do *something*. I'm afraid she will reach burnout and fade from the scene. Then what would I do? Who would bring my chocolate? Hey, I've gotten used to all the attention. She can't desert me now! How could I ever go back to being an ordinary person? How can I make her understand how much I'd love to have that new garbage disposal? How many paintings would it take to repay her generosity?

Lest I sound like the world's most manipulative, ungrateful friend, you have to know that all my friends are in on the secret. Each in her own way has asked to help and I can't refuse—can I?

Take the high school friend who operates a bed and breakfast in a small town about three hours from my house. Christmas has become her assignment. She arrives to help me put up the tree and decorate. We enjoy the time together immensely, but it is one of those guilt/gratitude situations. I know she spends the previous two months preparing her B&B for Christmas before coming to my house on the brink of exhaustion to help me. She knows that without her help I couldn't decorate for Christmas (I have to use my energy to paint after all). And she knows that when we are finished, there will be another task that "magically appears."

Did I really rope her into helping upholster a fabric headboard in one room? Did I wickedly drag her to the wallpaper store to make a selection for my bathroom? (That reminds me, as I write this, Christmas is coming and that wallpaper is still rolled up in the closet.)

Do you think a nice painting for her B&B will buy me some respectability?

The Great Chemo Excuse

Then there's all the stuff you don't have to do that you never wanted to do in the first place. How about your spouse's office parties? (You'd rather stay home and clean out the attic.) Or how about dinner with the boss and that dreadful bore he calls a wife? You put on your friendliest face and do your best to follow her insipid conversation, but instead you find yourself calculating the square root of the chair legs in the restaurant. You're not concerned she'll read this book, however. She hasn't read anything in years.

Guess what? For this and all other events to be avoided, you now have *The Great Chemo Excuse!*

Chemo Clubbers, you never ever again *have* to do anything you don't want to do, and you will be met only with understanding and sympathy. What happens when you must cancel out on a social engagement at the last minute? Fourteen boxes of chocolate and six florist deliveries show up at your door the next day. This chemo thing is really working, you think smugly.

My blessed, educated, and cultured husband absolutely loves the opera. While I respect and admire the opera, they still don't have recliners in the second row balcony. I'd rather stay home and clean the oven. So guess who never goes to the opera anymore? "Oh, I'd love to," I murmur sincerely, fluttering my eyes for just the right effect. (Don't forget to drop the voice here to a near death rattle, and let the words trail off a little.) "No, honey," he says, lovingly tucking me into bed. "You'd better stay home and rest. I'll go by myself this time." Wicked beast that I am, I sneak off to my art studio as soon as his exhaust fumes have cleared the driveway. I'll be back in bed before he returns with a delicious dinner he picked up on the way home. In spite of it all, I think he still loves me.

We've all been to those New Year's Eve parties that cease to be fun by 11 PM, at which point everyone just stands around getting drunk and trying desperately to appear as though they're having a good time. You need a Class "A" Emergency to leave early. Chemo Clubbers, no longer do you have to sneak off to another room and activate the fire alarm when you're ready to escape. You simply stand up and yawn. Everyone thinks you are so brave for even coming that they promise to drop off all kinds of goodies the next day. Chemo Clubbers, you are free at last!

I completely understand that you would rather be tongue-tied and toe-strung than go with your best friend to that "Creative Uses for Coffee Grounds" workshop next week. I am confident that soon you'll heed my advice and call her; gasping for breath and with a dreary voice, you'll explain that your doctor has scheduled you for a Purpleoctomy Gorgonzola next week.

Gentlemen Clubbers, you too are off the hook when your next-door neighbor enthusiastically offers you a free ticket to the "Understanding Your Weed-Eater" seminar. He explains that it's only a three-hour drive and you can ride along with him and his (dolt) brother. He assures you his two-year-old twins won't be a problem at all (he's agreed to take them off his wife's hands for the day). You don't have to tell me how convincingly "disappointed" you'll be as you play the chemo card.

The possibilities are endless as you gain confidence and explore the many benefits of the Great Chemo Excuse. Chemo

Clubbers, we have enough to put up with. Let's be shameless and have fun!

The Great Floral Phenomenon

Everyone wants to feel needed. We all want to be recognized for having been productive in some special way. For me, I take great pride in being personally responsible for the rise and fall of the floral market in recent years. I nod knowingly as I read in *The Wall Street Journal* that floral futures have increased sharply immediately following one of my surgeries. I learned that those who make a living by trading in this commodity study the weather patterns in Florida, California, and South America in order to predict prices. But I'm convinced that they also call my hospital to see if I've been admitted recently or if I am scheduled for another "slice and dice." All of this is due again to that army of wonderful, caring, and irreplaceable friends.

Just so you know I'm not completely shameless, I do take care of these friends when I'm having a "vertical" day. It has become part of my therapy to come up with creative ways to repay their generosity. For instance, it's easy to call a courier service and send my friends the beautiful bouquets of flowers I've received (not their own, of course). Creative recycling can be quite rewarding. They're happy. I'm happy. Plus, I get to enjoy the flowers for a couple of days and don't have to call Tidy Dumpster to haul away all the vases. It's a beautiful day for everyone!

If you're too respectable to use the recycling tip (probably not though, if you're reading this book), another idea would be to send someone to express your gratitude at the next get-together. Singing telegram? Cowboy Bob? String quartet? Belly dancer? You are limited only by your imagination and ingenuity. Just be sure you know your audience.

There is no doubt you could build a float for the Rose Bowl Parade with the flowers I've received over the past few years. But, remember, flowers don't just show up all by themselves. People have to *know* you're going into the hospital. Thank goodness for e-mail, which means hitting one button on your computer to send hospital e-mail alerts to everyone. People all over the world will know simultaneously that it's time to send flowers!

Learn to recognize another devious benefit from all those flowers. All the doctors and nurses who enter your room will recognize it as a "Malpractice Alert Zone." They'll immediately assume anyone with that many caring friends can afford an expensive army of Tasmanian Devil attorneys! Your medical care will be swift, sure, and friendly.

Queen Bee Syndrome

My husband and I recently went to a neighborhood café for dinner, and when we walked through the front door half the people in the restaurant jumped up to greet us. Curious strangers wondered in loud whispers *who* we were, convinced we were celebrities. Little did they know I'd just had another surgery and that my friends who happened to be there couldn't believe I was even standing up. I began to realize why people sometimes fake illnesses to the point of requiring hospitalization. When you are constantly pampered, coddled, and catered to, who wants to be normal?

I'm actually beginning to worry that all of these nutritional supplements and alternative witch doctor remedies might actually work. Egads, what if these nuclear wastes that I'm marinating in can actually reduce my tumors? It's bad enough that I might have to start fending for myself, but who will support the flower growers in South America? Besides, I haven't been to the grocery store in three years. I *hate* grocery shopping! I'd rather do chemo. Now I'm becoming alarmed. I think of all the things I've been avoiding—like paperwork.

I walked into my husband's office the other day and, although I could hear him, I couldn't see him. He was completely hidden behind a tidal wave of bills and forms on his desk. Hideous, life-threatening mountains of mind-numbing duties leaned precariously in dozens of stacks around the room. I stood there, distressed by the scene, and by the possibility that I could somehow get caught up in it. I moaned and grabbed my head, stricken with a sudden attack of Dementia Nervosa, and hurried from the room.

Queen Bee has gotten used to all the special treatment. How could I ever go back to being an ordinary person? I'd have to do ordinary things—such as touching up the shower grout. And heaven forbid I should ever have to start cooking again! All the planning, menus, shopping, preparation, cleanup. ARGH! That last thought was so depressing I had to go sit in my recliner and listen to comedy tapes for two hours to clear my head. I still shudder when I think of it.

I recently returned from my art studio and opened the garage door to park the car. As the interior of the garage came into view, I stared in disbelief at the devastation laid out before me. Had the overburdened shelving really collapsed, dumping those cans of paint all over the garage? I sat there blinking numbly, trying to make sense of it all. That was obviously a very important collection of used paint from the last several years. And now the various colors blended together on the garage floor, creating beautiful psychedelic patterns. (Leave it to an artist to see beauty in such devastation.)

Somehow, as the cans cascaded to the floor, they had managed to tip over the collection of furniture that was so carefully piled in the corner. Only that morning it had seemed too priceless to throw away. Now the broken bits of odds and ends lay strewn about in the paint. And why were the boxes scattered everywhere? They had seemed so happy and secure in that neat stack reaching to the ceiling. (Doesn't everyone need to keep extra boxes on hand? Who knows when you'll need to ship something to the kids?)

Okay, so things had gotten a little out of hand in the garage. As I picked my way through the debris, I remembered days of yore when I used to clean out the garage. I would ache up to my earlobes before the job was finished. And now this! I stumbled into the house and sank into my chair. Queen Bee couldn't possibly be expected to clean the garage. A mournful wail brought my husband racing into the room to feel my brow. Expressing alarm, he ran to get the thermometer. Luckily, I stopped him just in time before he thrust it under my tongue. I calmed his fears, explaining that it was just a momentary chemo flare. Chemo flare indeed! The thought of cleaning the garage was terrifying. I'd rather do chemo than clean out the garage!

Oops! This is *another* chapter my husband will never get to read.

Each one of us has a responsibility to examine our
personal situation and make the most
of our medical experience.

$ympathy $ales

I was stunned to learn that, statistically, only 30 percent of those with my level of cancer survive beyond five years, and so I decided to view this journey as a "character builder." It's been both amusing and amazing. In many ways, I've felt as though I'm riding an out-of-control bullet train rushing toward a rock wall. But living is about choices, the most important of which is choosing to live every moment to the fullest.

When the cancer verdict was handed down, we had five days before the surgeon would open me up and "clean house." Obviously, there were a lot of plans to be made and not much time; who knew what would be on the *other side* of surgery? Terrified, I sought refuge in my painting because it's the ultimate mental distraction. I had already started a new project and was determined to finish it before surgery. If it weren't for that deadline, I swear I would have jumped off a cliff.

When I came home from the hospital after surgery, my neighbor was one of the first people to arrive at my door bearing tokens of love. She was standing there with a pot (I swear it was as big as a washtub) filled with chicken and dumplings. If goodwill was going to fatten me up and make me healthy again, this was it. She brought it into my kitchen, and I immediately had a bowl. Delicious, hearty, and soul-nourishing as well. As we chatted, I was secretly calculating that it would take my family at least a month to eat all that she had brought!

When she was leaving, she spied the painting I had finished right before my surgery. I had brought it home from my studio and leaned it against a wall where it could dry undisturbed and out of the way.

"What's this?" she asked, looking it over. I told her about the painting and how I'd worked to finish it before going to the hospital.

"I love it!" she exclaimed. "If it's not already sold, I want to buy it."

"Why? It doesn't fit your house," I answered.

"Oh, it would too! And besides, I've always wanted one of your paintings. C'mon now, how much is it?"

When I told her, she insisted on picking it up the following week after I'd had a chance to get it framed.

"But don't you want to take it home first and see if it fits? And what about your husband? Don't you want to see if he likes it?"

"Oh, don't worry about him. He'll love it!" she insisted.

When she returned to pick it up, I told her I was pretty sure that was the most expensive pot of chicken and dumplings she'd ever made!

I'm delighted to report that she and her husband are happy with the painting, but I have to ask a question: would she have bought it if she hadn't seen the opportunity to own one of my paintings slipping away?

There have been other similar circumstances. Several years earlier, I had done a commissioned portrait of a woman's children. She'd occasionally mentioned doing a new one since her kids were older, but nothing had ever come of it. Now it seemed as though all of a sudden she wanted the portrait. After my operation she started bringing delicious stews and hearty meals to the house on a regular basis, each time inquiring about the possibility of a new portrait. By then I was in the thick of my chemo treatments and was painting only part-time. I couldn't promise when I could do it because portraits take a great deal of energy and thought. I swear, she was afraid I was going to die before I got around to her portrait.

Then it hit me: $ympathy $ales? It took almost a year, and it was a beautiful piece of work when I was finally able to paint it. I didn't want the galleries that carried my work, however, to know about my "medical issues." When people hear the word "cancer" they start to think of you as already dead, and there are a lot of artists out there ready to replace me. So I threatened dismemberment to anyone who dared mention my illness in any of the galleries! When one gallery hosted a one-woman exhibit, it was hard not to notice how sales of my artwork rose dramatically. I was surprised at how many acquaintances were all of a sudden buying my paintings. These people had known me and my artwork for years. Now I'll grant you in all humility that these were obviously beautiful and well-done paintings (artists are a modest lot), but why now? Every one of my oil paintings is produced by my hand, stroke by careful stroke. Shameless hussy that I am, I have to wonder what would be the various $ympathy $ales possibilities. The thought sends my devilish mind awhirl!

There is a lot of unused latent talent out there in Chemoland. We can only guess at the treasure trove of ingenuity lying wasted in recliners across the country, leaving $ympathy $ales untapped. I feel it is my duty to spark your imagination, Chemo Clubbers. I'd say there are no boundaries on what could be accomplished by a direct sales, one-person profit center. For instance, dietary supplements would be a natural for increasing your income, with a clever marketing program. Sales would be off the charts as you explained to your eager audience that you're a survivor due to these products. You were once horizontal, now you're vertical! You were once a pathetic, moth-eaten scrap of human garbage, but soon you'll be standing up, making regular trips to the hardware store to remodel your home. The orders resulting from $ympathy $ales would max out the local warehouse and put a strain on the national supply chain.

Each one of us has a responsibility to examine our personal situation and make the most of our medical experience. Therefore, I am going to be smart about my next O.R. event. I plan to have several of my paintings delivered to my hospital room. Invitations will be mailed and flyers will be posted throughout the hospital, ensuring an impressive attendance. The exhibit will coincide with my being rolled into the room, zoned out on morphine and moaning in agony. Digital monitors over my bed will give up-to-the-minute readouts on the chances of my survival. Do you think this would be pushing the limits of $ympathy $ales?

Chocolate
Helps
Everyone
Most
Of the time

You track your blood tests more closely
than you track the Dow Jones or the Nasdaq.

You Know You're on Chemo If . . .

You get up in the morning and your hair doesn't.

❧

You talk to your IV pole more than you talk to your kids.

❧

On a windy day, you find yourself grabbing your wig instead of your skirt.

❧

You track your blood tests more closely than you track the Dow Jones or the Nasdaq.

❧

You can't wait to get up in the morning to see if your face is red, green, or blue.

❧

You win a Nobel Prize for absorbing more toxic wastes than the state of Nevada.

❧

Your bookie places bets on how long it takes the nurse to find a vein in your arm.

You build your retirement plan with the money you
save on haircuts and mousse.

❧

You stay in shape with yoga because it's the most exercise you'll
ever get lying down (without having a cigarette afterwards).

❧

You win the Chemo Overachiever Award for the most
allergic reactions to chemotherapy.

❧

Your brain is so fried you write your kids' names on sticky
notes and put them all around the house.

❧

You make a needlepoint cover for your recliner and a
matching one for your head.

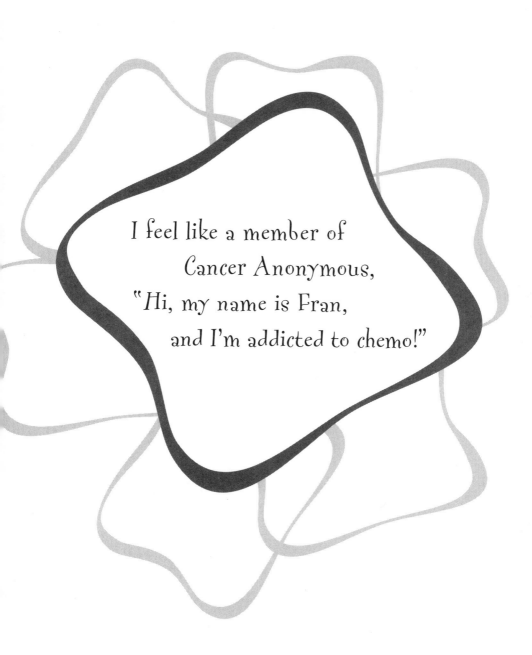

I feel like a member of
Cancer Anonymous,
"Hi, my name is Fran,
and I'm addicted to chemo!"

We usually look like a couple of drunks
staggering along, and it's hard to
tell who's holding up the other.

chapter 3

Have You Met My Friend Ivy?

I vy and I have a history. We've laughed, we've cried, we've walked a hundred miles together. Granted, we're not exactly the Bobbsey Twins (Ivy's a bit taller than I am). Still, we do have many things in common. We're both trim except for the significant bulges in our midsections. We both have bags under our eyes and neither of us has hair. She and I both tend to screech annoyingly when we're . . . well . . . when we're alarmed. Sometimes Ivy just gets tired of being ignored and makes a lot of noise for attention, as do I.

Her one distinctive feature, which causes people to stare, are her huge spreading toes. They provide her with some stability on our walks, but thresholds and other such impediments can cause her to stumble. We usually look like a couple of drunks staggering along, and it's hard to tell who's holding up the other.

I just wish she didn't have to accompany me *every* time I go to the ladies' room or to the shower. I enjoy my independence and find her constant companionship somewhat annoying. Frankly, sometimes I'd like to push her down the elevator shaft. This would have already happened except for one fact: when she made that sudden stop at the bottom, I'd be right there beside her. Thanks to a tangled web of tubing I'm tethered to Ivy, my IV pole.

Ivy and I get to spend lots of time together because of my body's ever-inventive way of confounding the medical community. Perhaps my body's most annoying habit (other than growing industrious cancer colonies) is finding a way to take me to the hospital on the "feel-good" days of my chemo cycle. So here I am, vertical for a change, but incarcerated and chained to Ivy. Sometimes we fight to see who gets to be boss for up to two weeks at a time! She's lazy, stubborn, dim-witted, and controlling. I am tyrannical, demanding, and bigger. Therefore, I usually win, even if it takes me longer to get there.

I have always enjoyed being active, and tennis is my favorite sport. Before cancer (B.C.), I used to play two or three times a week. On the intervening days I jogged. My legs, used to getting a lot of attention, are somehow unaware of the battle raging upstairs and have no appreciation for the fact that the rest of my body wants to melt into the mattress. My legs itch and twitch and whine and complain until the rest of my parts pull it together and agree to accompany them for a walk. So there go my legs, like a happy, energetic pup straining at the leash, pulling his baggy-eyed, soggy-faced human behind him. Sometimes it's just down the hall. Hey, it takes a lot of negotiating to get all my body parts to agree on just this one issue!

SURVIVAL SECRET THREE

Exercise Your Body

Yes, I know you feel dastardly! But you must help your body maintain some strength. Even if you do only yoga stretches lying down or sit on a reclining bicycle, the benefits are marvelous.

Exercise, like laughter, results in energy (even if you have to take a nap afterwards). Recently I conducted my own "clinical research," with some interesting results. I was prescribed a chemo drug that promised to scar and damage my heart muscle. Despite having no documentation on the advantages of cardio-vascular exercise to prevent this, I decided to maintain a regular cardio workout whether I felt good or not. Over a six-month period I stuck to my regimen with iron-will determination, even perfecting the art of napping on the treadmill. I gradually increased my duration and stamina and, to everyone's surprise, the tests completed after six months of chemo showed my heart to be functioning *better* than before I started. Need I say more about the benefits of exercise?

Most chemo cycles have two phases: vertical and horizontal. On horizontal days, my legs sometimes wait patiently for their turn. But when it's time to be vertical, look out! My legs strain at Ivy's leash.

We're quite a sight on the tennis court, dashing back and forth. Ivy's big toes get in the way as I dash for the impossible shot in the corner, and her black rubber wheels (not regulation for tennis courts) leave skid marks everywhere. As I rush forward for the net shot, Ivy lurches and cartwheels behind me, tubes flying and flailing wildly. Actually we make a good team, because her antics distract my opponent long enough for me to score some points with deadly corner shots.

With her help, I finally have control of the game. Left alley, right corner, lining up for the killer smash. I use my opponent for

We're quite a sight on the tennis court,
dashing back and forth!

target practice as Ivy screeches, careens, teeters, and sprawls out flat, trying to hold all her valves and tubes and screws together. She slides face down across the court, clearing bugs and leaves from my path. Meanwhile, I'm leaping, swinging, dodging tubes. Right-hand bullet! Backhand slice! By now, a crowd has gathered to witness the spectacle. As I prepare to execute a game-ending lob, Ivy drags behind me screeching her complaint. One of her bags has hit the court with a splat and split open. Ivy loses her fluids and I lose the point.

Now it's my opponent's turn to serve. I try to keep Ivy upright on her wheels so we can dash for the shot. I don't have time to position my racket, so I push Ivy's battery in front of the ball. Amazingly, it produces a short drop shot just over the net, and we win the point! I hear gasps from the gallery of spectators, one of whom loudly questions the legality of the point. I sense trouble when I see someone sprint for the pro shop to look it up in the rule book.

Ivy stands still (she's good at that), grateful to rest for a moment while I ace two serves in a row. I'm about to win this set, if only Ivy would stop crying. The crowd is becoming restless, indignant actually. Some are beginning to accuse me of unfair and unsportsmanlike strategy. Uh-oh, I'm in trouble. Here come two hunks in "regulation whites" trotting out of the pro shop. I try to ignore them as they stride onto the court to stop the game. It's Ivy's fault, I protest. Her battery, which monitors the flow through the tubes, never fails to start that irritable beep-beep-beep and this is driving my opponent crazy. Heck, it drives *me* crazy!

Okay, okay. I yawn and sit up in bed. "Shut up, Ivy!" I moan at her. Reality dawns as the nurse comes into my room and pushes the proper buttons to start a new bag of fluid. Rats! And we were winning, too.

It's "vertical" week, and I am in the hospital tethered to Ivy while my legs are screaming for exercise. As soon as the nurse departs, the rest of my body holds an emergency summit conference and everyone agrees to hit the hall in a serious way.

Did you know it's possible to "power walk" with an IV pole? I know I had you going with that tennis thing, but this time it's real. A word of caution to the fainthearted: you really have to know your equipment here. In true IV power walking, Ivy's toes and your toes sometimes miss each other by only a hair's width. This takes more precision than a Blue Angels maneuver. Ivy has six toes that spread out to form a circle. To start, you have to rotate the pole so that when you step forward in a long gait your toes will miss hers.

Trust me, this is not as easy as it sounds. In fact, I usually go home with black and blue toes. I have to hide them from my doctor, or she'll think it's another kinky side effect from chemo and order more tests.

Anyhow, after figuring out your alignment, position one hand around Ivy's neck in a death grip, your arm braced against her battery. If she goes over, it jerks a hole in your skin wherever the IV needle is inserted. Lastly, gather up the tangled length of tubing and hold it tightly in your free hand. That's your last chance to pull her upright and protect your IV needle. This isn't just a walk, it's a white-knuckle flight!

I have a great hospital. The carpeted halls impress the guests and probably attract new doctors, but it's hell for power walkers who take Ivy along. Not only doesn't she roll as well as you'd like, but the whole undertaking is downright dangerous.

Timing becomes another important factor. Avoid attempting your power walk right after breakfast when all the tortured victims on a hospital floor are *forced* to walk. They agreed to this when they initialed the "Patient Persecution Clause" at check-in. I've been there too, laboring over every move, so I try not to terrorize these souls. After breakfast, every piece of hospital equipment in the medical center inventory is pushed into the halls. In other words, it's rush hour on the floor. Bad time to attempt your power walking.

When most other patients are back in bed, however, and the hospital equipment has melted back into the walls, it's show time! Incorporating all the techniques described above, Ivy and I develop a head of steam. Hospital corridors, usually long rectangles, provide what I call "around the park." One complete lap takes me back to my room. The entire floor becomes my personal Indianapolis 500. Nurses know to step out of my way. Other patients stare in disbelief. Ivy and I are an impressive sight as we dash down the hall around corners, dodging carts, equipment, and other poles with humans attached. I tell you, we're fast! We once nearly outran a group of doctors answering a Code Blue. Of course, there's an ulterior motive here. If I can time my lap so my doctor catches me charging around the park, maybe she'll see how healthy I am and send me home.

It's a good theory anyway. Unfortunately, such demonstrations have never had much impact on my incarceration. While my doctor may be impressed with my velocity and endurance during these sprints, she's always more concerned about some annoying blood clot in my neck.

One time I was so frantic to get home and paint, I suggested to her that I could take Ivy apart, go home for some supplies, then come back and paint in my hospital room. It was day nine. Belligerence was setting in. Indeed, the maintenance department, increasingly tired of being pestered about greasing Ivy's wheels, finally left a can of spray lubricant in my room. My daily excursions around the park were leaving permanent ruts in the new hall carpet. In quiet desperation, I grabbed my doc with one hand, grabbed Ivy with the other, and shouted, "Find a way to get me out of here or this pole and I are going over the wall, baby!" Miraculously, by the next day my blood thinned adequately and I was sent home, sans Ivy.

The editor
told me this book had
too many exclamation points,
which were like shouting. I replied that
I spent the last five years trying to change
my life from a question mark to an
exclamation point. I had just
"aced" another vicious
surgery, and I like
shouting!

You have entered a TOXIC ZONE,
and meltdown of your car could result.

Bumper Stickers for Chemo Clubbers

- MY WIFE AND MY MONEY GO TO CHEMO

- WARNING—CHEMO BRAIN DRIVER ON BOARD!

- HONK IF YOUR HAIR FELL OUT TODAY

- MY OTHER HOME IS A HOSPITAL

- HONK IF YOU LOVE BALD MEN
  (TWICE IF YOU LOVE BALD WOMEN)

- OUT OF MY WAY! IT'S A VERTICAL DAY AND I'M HEADED
  FOR THE MALL!

- PARDON MY DRIVING—I'VE BEEN MARINATING

- CHEMO-SHMEMO. I'M STANDING UP!

- WARNING: IF YOU CAN READ THIS, YOU'RE FOLLOW-
  ING TOO CLOSELY. YOU HAVE ENTERED A TOXIC ZONE,
  AND MELTDOWN OF YOUR CAR COULD RESULT

- HOW'S MY DRIVING? CALL 1-800-MARINATE

- I'M ON CHEMO. WHAT'S *YOUR* EXCUSE?

Hairless makes life free and easy. Rose Glow,
a top-selling favorite, would add soft
peachy rose petals to the scalp.

chapter 4

Efficiently Hairless

I 'll no doubt be in the minority on this one, but I think losing your hair is one of the greatest benefits of chemo. Why all the hullabaloo about this little side effect? Not once have I seen anyone admit the *real* truth: being hairless makes life free and easy. It's the simplest of all physical conditions to correct. Heck, Hollywood has been doing wigs for decades.

I respect the fact that many societies around the world place great importance on women's hair—by insisting they cover it up. Just think of the freedom that would be afforded this suffocating femininity if they were simply and suddenly bald. One day, a progressive women's movement will begin providing chemo to the entire female population. There will be nothing left to talk about.

Our own American culture also makes a lot of noise about hair. The katrillion-dollar industry thrives on selling hair products that were produced for five cents and sold for thirty dollars, part of which goes to the zillion-dollar advertising campaigns. Have you noticed (believe me, when you're bald you notice) all the TV commercials for hair products? Entire magazines are devoted to hair care and related products. Did you know that practically none of the smiling, young beauties in either TV or magazine ads displays her own hair? Wigs, hairpieces, and hair weaving rule. Except for those few who were born "follically" advantaged, all kinds of trick lighting and fans embellish what would otherwise look like a mop.

We are a media-driven society. If a leading designer hair-product company introduced something like Chrome Glow for bald heads, their ad campaign would have an entire nation applying razor to scalp. Think of it. True Blue Chrome Glow and Chrome Glow Glitter. Rose Glow, a top-selling favorite, would add soft, peachy rose petals to the scalp. The possibilities are endless. Even now I can sense your excitement as your bleary chemo brain conjures up dazzling, artistic, custom-made designs.

Where once we flocked to beauty salons for hair coloring and cutting, we would now go in equal if not greater numbers for head shaving, waxing, and designer applications by Chrome Glow and its explosion of competitors. After all, no one wants to stop going to the beauty salon. Someone might think we have more time for baking, washing baseboards, and trimming the hedges.

As the trend catches on in the fashion world and the runways of Paris and Milan, enterprising salons might actually begin offering chemo as a service. *No razors, no stubble, and it's long-lasting.* Where once you dropped a paltry $200 at the salon, now they can charge the full $6,000 infusion rate.

Wig shops will quickly adjust as they phase out their hapless hairpieces to begin stocking alluring and diverse selections such as Pearl-Studded Chrome Glow and Ready-Confetti. It's a win/win situation. No more will women worry about their coiffure in the wind with non-wind-reactive Chrome Glow. Umbrella? Forget it. Chrome Glow is waterproof for easy swimming and showering.

Finally, you gentlemen Chemo Clubbers will have real options in the doorknob department. What about Daytona

Chrome Glow for the racy look, Rocky Mountain Chrome Glow (complete with evergreen flecks) for the outdoorsman, and Chrome Glow Concerto for the sophisticates and cultured types? Singles bars will jump on the bandwagon with convenient spray cans in the restrooms for quick fixes.

Come on, you investors and entrepreneurs. Where are you? I'm too busy here painting to take advantage of this one. Wait a minute. Chrome Art! I could paint a beautiful floral arrangement on your head. You could choose Rembrandt or Monet. Progress is borne by the next great idea, and I'm handing this one to you on a silver platter. Get busy!

Sorry, I was on a roll there and lost myself in the excitement. Let me point out the other advantages of being hairless, such as having no need to shave those areas where we have unwanted hair. And think of the savings on water now that you aren't shampooing.

My former prep time for going out included an hour of showering and shampooing, or at least long enough to empty a thirty-gallon hot water tank. Needless to say, my husband loves my hairless condition because he no longer has to shower in cold water. For me, it's now a two-minute deal tops. Suds up, rinse off, exit. A little makeup, plop on the wig, and I'm out of there. With the time I once spent coaxing my uncooperative hair into tortured arrangements, I can now produce three more paintings a month. (With that added income, no wonder he likes me hairless!)

Recently we were packing for a weekend getaway. After I'd dragged out the suitcase, I realized I had nothing to put in it. No razor, foam, dryer, shampoo, conditioner, curlers, mousse, spray, gel, hand mirror, brushes, combs, clips, and no shower cap. With an exhilarating sigh of freedom, I plopped on my ever-ready wig, threw an extra blouse and slacks in my husband's bag, and I was ready to leave.

I've gotten so used to being hairless that I've become quite nonchalant about it; maybe even careless. Why should I don my wig for the repairman or delivery guy? They're focused on their schedules and don't give a hoot. Besides, in the summer it's way too hot to wear *anything* on your head. If I'm out doing errands on a hundred-degree day, I'll frequently take off my wig in the car. Why should I try to impress the fellow in the car next to me at the red light? I saw him picking his nose and talking on the phone. Does he care?

One hot day, I was preparing dinner (yes, I do cook . . . *occasionally*) and realized that I needed some fresh basil from our herb garden on the patio. Without looking first, I dashed out the door. The noise of the door slamming behind me attracted the attention of four men jogging by. I saw their heads swivel abruptly as the joggers all stared openly at my bald head. I realized it would look even more ridiculous to suddenly dart back in the house, so I threw my chin in the air and marched toward the basil. It was their problem, not mine. I stifled a giggle as I saw one of them stumble.

So, what is hair but what we make it? Are we so fragile that our whole self-esteem is based on a rowdy thatch of fuzz sprouting from the top of our heads? Sure, have a few wigs for fun. Be a different person daily. And when you feel like it take it off and go natural.

My hair has come and gone so many times, it stays confused. But it always grows back in with wonderful curls, which I refer to as my $150,000 perm. It's kind of like that rainbow after a storm, a reward for your endurance.

Wondering if they would miss me, I
decided to crawl under the operating table.

chapter 5

O.R. Guest Register
(Slice and Dice Record)

E arlier, I warned you about my warped and wicked sense of humor. If you've read this far and still harbor any doubts about that, this chapter will erase them all. However, you will come to understand my ulterior motive.

I checked in for surgery the first few times wearing a sweat suit. As I sat in the surgical lounge waiting for vivisection, it occurred to me that *there must be a better way*. This thought intensified in the Preoperative Zone, where I lay on the narrow bed feeling like a trussed turkey headed for the dinner table. My father always said, "There is an art to everything, even shoveling dirt." The path was clear. I vowed that next time (in my case there is always a next time), I would do this differently.

What if, when I check in for the next surgery, the high school marching band accompanies me? They're a spirited group and always in need of more practice. I envision them playing trombones, trumpets, tubas, bass drum—you name it. Just imagine the happy scene as our procession enters the hospital lobby, the reflection of the brilliant overhead lights bouncing off all that gleaming brass! Think of all that noise reverberating off the marble floors and tiled ceilings. Picture if you will the brightened expressions on the otherwise ashen-faced patients as they spring to their feet, join us in a conga line, and march gaily around the lobby! Hundreds of people would come running from every office and cubicle to view the spectacle. Can't you just see the frenzy as wheelchair attendants hustle their wild-eyed passengers to safety from the oncoming band?

Just imagine the president of the hospital marching angrily in our direction, followed by a cadre of security personnel. Just then the SWAT team with full riot gear dashes in and begins shouting orders through megaphones!

Okay, so it's a bad idea. Anyway, as they roll me into surgery I would still be giggling. They'd have to start my sedation early, and I think even the surgeon would need a martini to calm things down. I explained my plan to the doctor, but she suggested something more dignified. I promised I'd give it some thought. The U.S. Marine Honor Guard would be a big hit. They practice their marching drill for months on end and seldom get to show off. All one hundred of them with their impressive uniforms and white gloves certainly could add a festive air to any drab hospital lobby. Don't you think those stuffy guys from security would stand at attention as we pass by? I'll bet I could even secure the plushy corner room the next time I check in.

Of course it's clear that most of my ideas would land me in a padded room instead. I know, but it's fun to visualize, don't you think? By the time I was planning my new check-in procedures, I had already experienced surgeries one through nine. They included the standard ins and outs. You know: ports in, ports out, gadgets in, tumors out. Missing in action: ovaries, uterus, omentum, appendix, breast, navel, colon, and a bushel basket of tumors. Suffice it to say I have more zippers than a bomber jacket.

Add to this list a lot of complications. I call myself the *what if* person. What if this happens or what if that happens? I am the one the *what ifs happen* to, the leftover percentage that always falls through the statistical cracks. We all need to stand out at something.

After the tenth surgery, I decided it was time to stop complaining and start bragging. In a conversation with my surgeon, I remarked that so many people had put their hands in my guts I was thinking of starting a guest register for the operating room. She dared me to do it. (You can see why we get along.)

I accepted her challenge by buying an attractive guest register in appropriate hospital white. With a red paint pen (what better color to use?) I wrote on the front, "Fran's O.R. Guest Register." Inside the cover I inscribed, also in red: *This book is dedicated to all who have placed their hands or other medical devices in Fran's guts. Please sign in and happy hunting!* Then I listed the basic information of all past surgical visits. The doctors love it that I refer to surgery as "Slice and Dice."

Each page was numbered in red. I listed the procedure performed, the lead surgeon, the hospital, and what type of anesthesia was used. I have the surgeon autograph beside his or her name. All nurses, technicians, and the anesthesiologist also sign in.

It was an instant hit. All the nurses and technicians in Pre-Op and Recovery love to sign in. IV nurses know that if they hit the mark on the first attempt, they get a gold star by their name. A little incentive never hurts!

I roll into surgery with the book lying on my chest and make everyone in the room promise not to let me leave without it. An interesting point: some surgeons prefer to sign after the procedure is over. They don't want to "jinx" the surgery. Nothing like knowing that your surgeon is superstitious!

Always one to push the limits a little further, I also made a T-shirt. At the time I'm writing this book, I've completed a lifetime tally of nineteen visits to the O.R. I have been in six hospitals in my city, all of them more than once. I go to the hospital the way some people go to lunch. In the last few years, I've been going to Zale-Lipshy University Hospital. On the front of my T-shirt I have emblazoned in large letters, *Zale-Lipshy Frequent Flier*. On the back it says, *ZLUH I'm a repeater!* Not all that original, I'll admit, but terribly amusing to everyone in the Admissions Office, Patient Services, and Pre-Op.

When I check into the hospital, it's as if my husband and I are at a party. We greet all the staff, hug, and laugh like old friends reunited. The other Slice and Dice victims waiting their turn stare at us in disbelief. Some scene! The nurses preparing me for surgery get a big kick out of the shirt and go tell other nurses who come in to get a glimpse and chuckle. As you know, custom dictates that you check in as God created you with all clothing thrown unceremoniously into a plastic bag. A lot of folks show up in their bathrobes. I have my own uniform—the T-shirt and blue jeans. When I'm preparing to leave the hospital, we wheel out with the same ceremony.

Let's face it. I think laughter works for everyone, including medical staff. Besides, somewhere in my soul I believe that it's harder not to do your best for a person who makes you laugh.

I also have a fun checklist for the team working in the operating room. They are usually scurrying around attending to their respective duties. Once, while lying there on the table, I felt like another piece of medical equipment. Wondering if they would miss me, I decided to crawl under the operating table. That caused a great deal of anxiety among the team members! So now I stay on the table, but I ask them to answer the following qualification quiz:

1. Did everyone get a good night's sleep?
2. Did anyone have a fight last night with his or her spouse, etc.?
3. Did everyone have at least one but not more than three cups of coffee today?
4. Did anyone have a car wreck on the way to work this morning?

They love to joke around, and the answers usually come back:
1. No
2. Yes
3. No
4. Yes

All of this is a great stress reliever. I used to go in with butterflies in my already-hungry tummy and in a full-body sweat. I would lie in Pre-Op with my fists clenched until my fingers turned blue. Now, instead of contemplating my life (or possible lack thereof) with eyes glazed over, I've created the best party atmosphere I can concoct without getting arrested. Security does not look at me suspiciously, and the guys with the straitjackets don't meet me at the door. What we do is laugh, chat, visit, and take all the stress out of the air. Instead of sitting there teary-eyed and tense, my husband joins in the amusement. I don't need tears right now. I need laughs and backbone.

Perhaps you are just starting your journey. With a little luck, you'll never need the O.R. Guest Register I've included in the back of this book for your convenience. Or maybe you creative types would rather have your own custom-embroidered, gold-plated, hoity-toity, rootin'-tootin' version complete with hospital cartoons. It's a way to distinguish yourself from the multitude of other patients. Then when you push the call button everyone will come running.

You were asked to hold the scissors at the
ribbon-cutting ceremony for the new hospital.

Your Medical Bills Are Too High If . . .

Your doctor has opened a satellite office on the beach in Tahiti.

$$$

The chemo clinic was completely outfitted in gold-plated IV poles in your honor.

$$$

You were asked to hold the scissors at the ribbon-cutting ceremony for the new hospital.

$$$

There's a bronze statue of you in the hospital lobby.

$$$

The Fed lowers interest rates to help you cover your debt.

$$$

Your hospital bills are etched in crystal and mounted on marble pedestals.

$$$

Your nurses are adorned with uniforms handmade in Italy.

$$$

The valet at the medical center bought fuzzy dice for your car.

$$$

Your spouse has a vibrating recliner in the
hospital's waiting room.

$$$

The hospital installed a curbside
"Express Check-In Booth" just for you.

$$$

You qualified for the National Disaster Relief Fund.

$$$

Your insurance company sent you a DO-IT-YOURSELF
MEDICAL KIT, complete with scalpel, sutures, and drop cloths.

I guess you could call me a "Million Dollar Babe." The only reason I'm still here is because this body is like an old bottle of fine wine: you know it's past its prime, but there's too much invested in it to throw it out.

My friends were as tenacious at feeding me
as they were on the tennis courts.

chapter 6

Death by Casserole

You already know that I have been blessed with an abundance of wonderful, generous friends who have taken care of me in endless ways throughout chemo. But I realize I haven't said nearly enough about FOOD.

These friends have taken it upon themselves to feed me and my family through all my cancer crises. These ladies played tennis with me (I wisely let them win), and now they are showing their gratitude by keeping me supplied with a constant flow of fabulous cuisine.

A pearl of wisdom here: in your retirement plan under the heading "Long-Term Care" should be a whole section dedicated to building your support team. To begin the section there should be a recommendation that whatever your interest, be it golf, dirt bike racing, or dog sledding, let your friends win a significant amount of the time! Perhaps they too will show their appreciation with gifts of homemade goodies.

My years of experience negotiating the chemo lifestyle can help put you on the fast track to greater chemo enjoyment and creative casserole use. For instance, let's say a chicken curry casserole finds its way to your doorstep one day. You don't really favor curry all that much, but those giant chicken breasts look promising. Just rinse them off and freeze them. Next week when the spaghetti sauce arrives, drop in the chicken breasts and simmer. Voilà! Chicken cacciatore. Magnifico!

Those in my wonderful support group (see how I continue to butter them up?) have actually divided up the calendar and organized a regular food-drop at my door. I was terribly humbled (no, really I was). I'm afraid I've been so irreverent about so many things up to now that you'll never believe when I'm serious. So let me try again. Seriously, I was terribly humbled by their acts of kindness and appreciative of their generosity.

You have to understand the level of their sacrifice. They're all empty-nesters, so most of them hadn't cooked in years except when their kids came home for the holidays. Suddenly, they were cooking for me. All over town, husbands were coming home to the unfamiliar smell of dinner on the stove. One guy got so excited his pacemaker went into red alert. More than one marriage took on a whole new glow because of me. Husbands were abandoning the golf course early; poker games were being canceled. One of these wives even got a new car for her birthday!

These ladies love to travel. One saint even came home from a trip, cooked me dinner, and left the very next day on another adventure. In shock, I wanted to let them off the hook. But I was somewhere between eternal gratitude and desperate need. My husband hadn't really come to grips with what was happening to us. Bless his heart, he was attempting to run his business and figure out his role as a caregiver all at the same time. He was embarrassed that people insisted on bringing us food (I think it's a guy thing) but grateful to sit down for a meal he didn't have to prepare himself at the end of a long day.

One friend we call Saint Katie delivered lasagna, salad, rum cake, and a bottle of wine the day I came home from the hospital after major surgery. I couldn't eat any of it, naturally, but my husband hadn't eaten a decent meal in more than a week. I was so grateful that he could relax for a moment.

My friends were as tenacious at feeding me as they were on the tennis court. Never once taking the fast-food cop-out route, they continued to drop off home-cooked extravaganzas. My protests redoubled their efforts. I was on their calendar and had a good thing going.

Afraid of being labeled a chemo scam artist, I decided to repay them for their kindness with a luncheon, where I thanked them profusely for their love and support, suggesting they should take a break. After an update on my treatment, I told them the truth: I was never going to get off chemo. The food kept rolling in.

Chemo Clubbers, I'm writing this book to help you make the best of your chemo experience and perhaps avoid some of the trouble spots. How harmless could it be to have a few friends dropping over some beef stew and cheesecake?

Now, if you have more than a few friends delivering food to your door, there will come a time when it could get out of control. Know the warning signs. You will see the foil wrappers overflowing your dumpster and blowing down the street. When you come home and find vagrants congregating in front of your house, you'll know that the word is out on the street that there is plenty to eat at your house. Hopefully, you won't get to the point I did—the guy on the local corner who usually advertises "Will Work for Food" started holding up a sign that said "Need a Ride to Fran's House." Before you know it, the local soup kitchen will begin advertising your house as their newest satellite location. From there it will only be a few days until the media arrive to check out what's going on, with lights and cameras capturing all of those yet-to-be-done home repairs on your "Things to Do While on Chemo" list.

Finally, one day hope will dawn. You'll get a phone call from your next delivery, who'll say she can't get down the street to your house because of the Port-O-Let truck (set up to handle the crowd), the fire and medical assistance trucks (just in case), the police squad (crowd control), and the mobile TV broadcast centers.

Try to be gentle as you explain that she can take you off her calendar. Point out that several concerned corporations have arrived to service your needs via the Pizza Hut trailer, the Coca-Cola van, the Good Humor truck, and various city-approved hot dog, pretzel, and taco carts.

Eventually the food will subside as you patiently coax these ladies out of their kitchens. Assure them their marriages will survive if they return to their garden/book/investment clubs. If necessary, start a vicious rumor that you've been miraculously cured and will soon be back playing tennis. Drastic needs call for drastic measures.

Put this one down on your Chemo Side Effects chart.

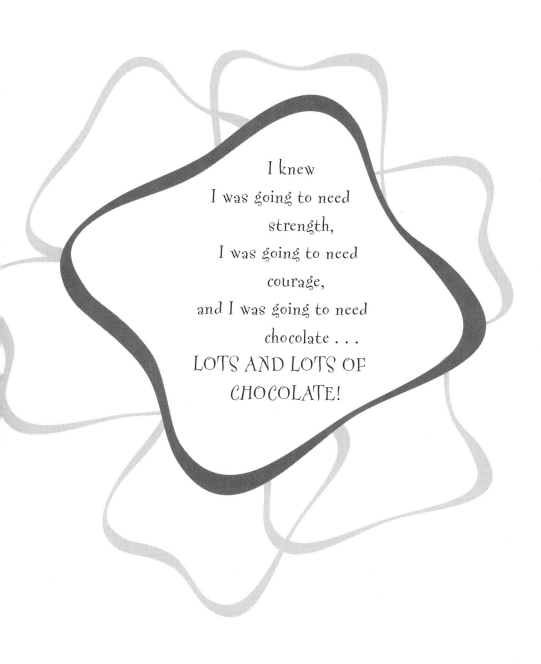

I knew
I was going to need
strength,
I was going to need
courage,
and I was going to need
chocolate . . .
LOTS AND LOTS OF
CHOCOLATE!

There is grass growing around your sofa,
and a tree has sprouted between your toes.

Signs You Were Asleep Too Long

There's moss growing on your blanket and
the country has elected a new president.

Your house was declared a state historical district.

Your family called in a team to have you surgically
removed from the sofa.

Your children mortgaged your house, left, and
joined a commune.

You received sixty-seven e-mail requests to buy your
auto because it turned into a classic.

The EPA declared your recliner an environmental hazard.

The state built a freeway over your house.

Your family mailed the last photo of you awake
to Ripley's Believe-It-Or-Not.

The Chemo Club awarded you the
Lifetime Achievement Award for Sleeping.

There is grass growing around your sofa, and
a tree has sprouted between your toes.

Neighborhood activists hauled your recliner to a
state-approved toxic waste dump, with you in it.

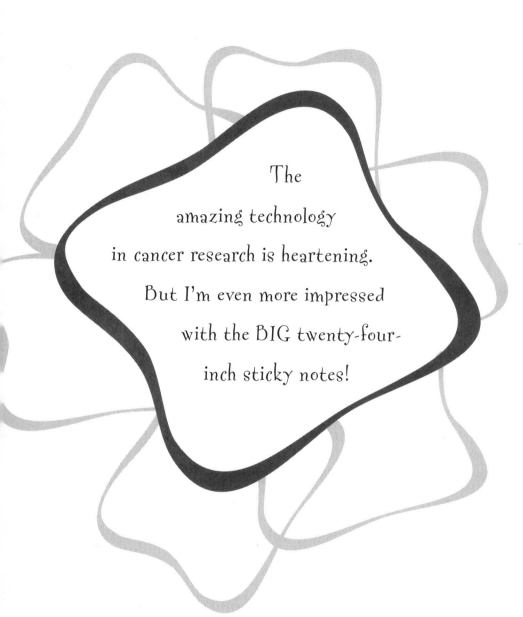

The
amazing technology
in cancer research is heartening.
But I'm even more impressed
with the BIG twenty-four-
inch sticky notes!

My wig fell haphazardly over my face, then
plopped out the window, and landed on his feet!

chapter 7

Brain (Dis)Connection
(Or "It's Not My Fault")

How many of my darkest secrets can I divulge and still be seen in public? How many errant misdeeds can one person blame on chemo? I can't think about myself. After all, I'm doing this for you, fellow Chemo Clubbers. If I carry the flag, then you can fall in behind me in absolute safety. If I bare all, then you can just point to this chapter and say, "See! It's not just me. It happens to all of us." This chapter will substantiate any act of stupidity; any paltry mistake will be instantly understood and forgiven by the offended party.

We in the exclusive Chemo Club know the term "Chemo Brain" is no joke. My brain, fried to a crisp like a tater tot left too long on the stove, makes doing important paperwork dangerous. Once, while writing checks, I accidentally sent the cable bill payment to my attorney and my attorney's payment to the cable company. The cable company showed up the next day (the first time I ever got a prompt response from them) with seventeen trucks and a cast of thousands, ready to custom-fit my home with a world-class system. All those vehicles blocked traffic on my street, and my neighbors, already irritated at the food caravan, filed yet another complaint.

When I forgot to mail the utility bills and the power was turned off, my husband assumed all paperwork duties.

This has happened to you, hasn't it? I wrote those bills; I know I did. We found them later in the pantry between the Cheerios and the peanut butter. I guess I needed a snack on the way to the mailbox.

It's not my fault, I pleaded. It was Chemo Brain.

There have been other episodes you may recognize. For instance, everyone finds the iron in the fridge now and then, right? And who among us hasn't accidentally put the ice cream in the pantry? It was just bad timing that we were leaving to visit my sister for the weekend. When we returned home, a puddle of ice cream met us at the door. Hey, the ants were happy.

Once when we were expecting another couple over for dinner, I brought home a wonderful, freshly prepared meal to serve them. When they were an hour late, I called them to see what the problem was. Oops! I'd never called to invite them. Chemo Brain.

Haven't you ever gone to yoga, put your purse in a locker, and then forgotten *which* locker? I actually tried to find it by using the little key in several locks. When it opened four lockers, all empty, I decided to wait it out. After all twenty-five people in the yoga class had cleaned out their lockers and left, I remembered with embarrassment that I hadn't used a locker. My purse, of course, was in the car, and the car keys were in my pocket.

Everyone locks the keys in the car, right? Well, after three such incidents in one week I tied a key under my rear bumper. This has to be carefully calculated—far enough under so the key can't be seen by just anyone, but not so far that you can't reach it easily in a rainstorm. (How do you think I learned that lesson?)

Forget the keys; how about losing the car? It happens to everyone, admit it. If the car gets left at the airport, the health club, or a friend's house, my long-suffering spouse usually doesn't complain. Recapture is possible without too much stress. How could he blame me? It's not my fault. Chemo Brain.

It must have been great when we used horses. They could find their way home by themselves.

One time I was preparing to go shopping and do some errands with our two young sons. They were so cute in their summer shirts, shorts, and socks. Problem was, that's all they were wearing. Halfway through the day, it dawned on me to ask them where their shoes were. Turns out we left home without shoes. (Hey, if Mom didn't care, why should they?) So far I've never lost the kids. I'm very proud of that accomplishment.

Recently, I even lost my husband. (This was *not* intentional. I like my husband, but hey, if you want to lose yours remember Chemo Brain.) Let me explain that we originally met at an airport when I was still flying. Now here we were back in the same airport thirty-two years later, separated and lost. It's a very long story, but suffice it to say that a security guard noticed my distress and offered to help me find my husband. Without even hesitating, I looked at the officer and replied, "No thanks. Eventually we'll bump into each other just like we did the first time." Chemo Brain was in control.

My family calls me the sticky-note queen. Sticky notes here, there, and everywhere—on my kitchen chair, my bathroom mirror, in the cupboard. Sticky notes on the dashboard, the porcelain figurine in the front entry, the back door. No place too remote, no item too sacred to be the bearer of a sticky note.

And then there was the incident with the kitchen. . . .

Once I was watering the plants and mixing something I thought was the appropriate fertilizer into the watering can. (By the way, all of my plants look as though they've been on chemo for decades.) Anyway, I was stirring and mixing, trying to get this stuff to dissolve—

What? Oh, you want to know about the kitchen incident? I'm sorry I mentioned it. I am writing this for your benefit, however, and some of you may need a really big Chemo Brain disaster to point to so that whatever stupid, whacked-out, idiotic stunt you pull will absolutely pale in comparison. Okay, my husband came home and found that I had accidentally (they're all accidents, aren't they?) put the car in the kitchen. It was completely understandable! Well, mistakes happen. Besides, I'd been trying to figure out how to lose the kitchen for years.

SURVIVAL SECRET FOUR

Don't Drive "Under the Influence"!

Driving while under the influence of toxic nuclear wastes can be dangerous. Unfortunately, I found that out the hard way; but I've only had one chemo-related car accident involving another person.

In my traffic accident, my reflexes were okay; it was just bad judgment. I made a right turn into the flow of traffic, failed to see an oncoming car, and sort of rubbed up against the car on my left. The other driver and I pulled over and jumped out to survey the damage. I looked at her vehicle in disbelief. God had obviously been shoving this poor woman in front of chemo patients for years. Her aged auto was already smashed, dented, scarred, and rusted from stem to stern. She smiled at me somewhat bemused.

"My car is okay, but yours is a mess," she offered. She was right. I had managed to scrape or dent every panel on that side of my car. I felt blessed relief that she wasn't injured and wasn't going to hold me liable.

"I have to get to the hospital," she said. "My husband has cancer and he's in bad shape." Funny how you can feel blessed relief and a crushing blow in the same instant.

I draped myself around her shoulders and whispered something woefully inadequate. I drove away stunned by the experience. Why had our Creator picked this poor soul for me to run into? Hadn't the woman suffered enough in her life without my involvement? The accident was clearly my fault. When I got home, I put a sticky note on the windshield: NO DRIVING AFTER MARINATING.

Thanks to Chemo Brain I'm always confusing my credit card for my driver's license. When a cashier asks how I'm going to pay, I invariably hand her my driver's license. She'll stand there with a blank look on her face, studying it. Then I realize my mistake and hand her my credit card. So, it was only natural when the police officer pulled me over that I dutifully stuck my credit card out the window as he approached. He immediately became indignant, and I searched my arsenal of chemo excuses to get me out of this. Should I show him my fresh road map of scars in a blatant play for sympathy? No, he'd accuse me of being obscene. Bad enough he probably thought I was trying to bribe him. Maybe I should show him my medical port and play the chemo card? He might add "driving under the influence" to whatever transgression I'd committed. So I did none of these things. Instead, I simply became flustered and my chin began to quiver (a personality defect I've had since birth).

As I scrambled for my driver's license and a tissue I tried to take off my sunglasses, but they got hung up in my wig. The wig fell haphazardly over my face for a moment and then plopped out the window, landing on his feet. Our eyes locked in a showdown. Mine were inquisitive, his were confused. He looked down at my wig draped over his boots. He obviously didn't want to touch it, and I was afraid to open the door to pick it up. Even a door handle seemed more machinery than I could handle at the moment. Suddenly I started to giggle. Then we were both laughing so hard that tears were rolling down our cheeks. I asked permission to open the door and retrieve the wig. Wiping his eyes, he admonished me to slow down and be careful. Was it an accident that my wig fell out of the car? I don't know. It just happened. But before I drove away, I put a sticky note on the dashboard (I keep a supply of them in the glove compartment): WHEN TROUBLE IS BIG, THROW OUT YOUR WIG!

In my own way, I've figured out a lot of the pitfalls caused by Brain (Dis)Connection. Here are some inevitable truths to ease your concerns and let you know that God takes care of those too forgetful to take care of themselves.

Tips for Chemo Brains

~ Can't remember if you brushed your teeth? Check to see if your toothbrush is wet.

~ Can't remember if you took your pills? If your toothbrush is lying beside the pill bottle, you probably did.

~ Can't find your toothbrush? Look near the pill bottle. (Are you beginning to see how easy this is?)

- Can't remember if you brushed your hair? Who are you kidding? You don't even remember the last time you had hair!

- Can't remember your doctor's appointment? Don't worry, your insurance will pay the bill anyway.

- Can't remember to set the alarm? What for? You'll be horizontal all week.

- Can't remember your kids' names? When they call for money, they'll remind you.

- Can't find your car keys? Then you need a nap, not a trip to the mall.

- Can't remember to put the leftovers away after dinner? No problem. It won't take so long to warm them up for lunch.

- Can't remember if you sent thank-you notes? Send a "thinking of you" card. They'll so admire your sensitivity that they'll probably bring over more chocolate.

- Can't remember where you put the chocolate? Are you crazy? No one ever has any leftover chocolate. You ate it *all*.

- Can't remember what day it is? Find a newspaper. And while you have it, read "Dear Abby" and the funnies. Abby will make you realize how easy your life is by comparison, and laughing at the funnies will make you feel better.

Think about it. You've needed a really solid excuse for years. Now you have one. Let's all be thankful for Chemo Brain. The sky is the limit on the havoc we can create while still maintaining our innocence!

You are definitely hyperneurotic if you think
you're going to use that thing on me!

Important Medical Terms

AGITATED—a state of restlessness. "The *agitated* patient in Room 37 tried to scratch out my eyeballs when I put his IV in."

AMBULATE—to get out of bed. For Chemo Clubbers this does not mean jogging, but rather creeping around, hunched over, moaning in agony.

ANESTHESIOLOGIST—the person who stands behind you passing gas.

ANTERIOR—the front. If you mistakenly put your gown on backward, you'll leave your *anterior* exposed.

CRYOGENICS—to freeze. "These chicken livers have been *cryogenized* too long."

DEBULKING—removing obnoxious, rancid objects. "I have to *debulk* the refrigerator."

HYPERNEUROSIS—a lot of nerve. "You are definitely *hyperneurotic* if you think you're going to use that thing on me!"

INTERVENTIONAL RADIOLOGY—the service that reams out arteries. "Honey, the drain is plugged up again. Better call *Interventional Radiology*."

LAPAROSCOPE—periscope down!

LUCID—to be awake or aware. "I hope the surgeon will be *lucid* for that 5:00 AM vivisection . . . and I hope I won't."

METASTASIZE—spreading to distant areas. "My surgically extracted body parts have all *metastasized* to little jars around the lab."

NEUROPATHY—numbing of the nerves. "My nurse exhibited obvious *neuropathy* while I screamed for food the last five days."

PATIENT—an impossibility. "The nose tube isn't coming out today. Just relax and be *patient*."

VIVISECTION—to slice and dice. "I'm *vivisecting* this roast so I can make stew."

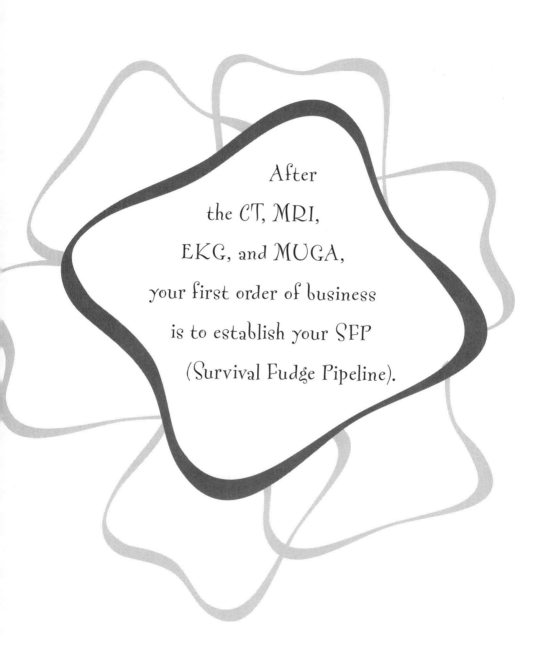

After
the CT, MRI,
EKG, and MUGA,
your first order of business
is to establish your SFP
(Survival Fudge Pipeline).

I fully intended to indulge in every luscious
temptation on the table without
making a spectacle of myself.

chapter 8

Automatic Weight Control

Are you beginning to see a pattern here? Chemo has lots of advantages. One of my favorites continues to be food. You already know that I am besieged with friends bearing food and chocolate and all kinds of goodies. The best part is that I can eat them all and not gain an ounce.

While many of my friends are desperately trying (or not trying) to lose weight, I am slim and trim—all thanks to chemo. Before cancer came to call, I too was fighting a losing battle against those nasty excess pounds. Slender in my youth, I discovered that every advancing year brought a few more permanent pounds. I've always been a very disciplined person and refused to give up on the weight control. Every bite that went into my mouth had to be measured and accounted for. I have been active my whole life and have a voracious appetite. My father used to say that some people eat to live, while others live to eat. I am definitely in the second category.

As a result, before cancer I had been hungry for twenty years, subsisting on green, crunchy things. I knew from experience that sinning one day would invariably show on the scales the next. At one point I tired of the battle and conceded a measure of defeat, glumly replacing my entire wardrobe with clothes a size larger—

everything from formal to tennis to loose-fitting jeans. I'll confess I kept a rack of "chick dresses" in the back of the closet that I refused to throw away. These are clothes I regard as "fifty going on fifteen," meaning only someone fifty years old who still wanted to be fifteen would wear them. (Please tell me that we all go through these growing pains, so I won't feel ridiculous.)

Before I knew it, however, all of the new clothes were out the window. Every belt was too short, every zipper too snug. Every piece of clothing squished and squeezed me. I was becoming both uncomfortable and impatient, so I swallowed my pride one more time and went shopping for the next size up. I hate shopping. It's tiring and time consuming. I'm finicky about fabrics and colors and always seemed to be out of step with the latest fashion trends. And the prices? They're enough to gag a goose. When the cabbage soup diet fad came along, it helped me avoid that next dreaded shopping torture and at least stay in the same (enlarged) size. I called myself the "Cabbage Soup Queen" because it worked wonders for me.

Do I look back now on those calorie-conscious days with any degree of fondness? No. Cancer and chemo are here to stay, so I might as well make the best of the situation (as I plop another scoop of ice cream into the hot fudge). At every step of the way these past several years, I've managed to maintain my appetite while actually using food as part of my reward system.

Most chemo drugs are given on a three-week cycle. After infusion, certain days fall into dependable patterns. For a few days I won't be interested in eating at all. Sort of like a bear in hibernation I sleep for days on end, eating with reckless debauchery when I awake. If things get out of hand and the weight starts creeping back I don't worry, because as surely as God made little kittens I'll be back in surgery soon. Even a quick day surgery is good for a five pound loss! Thanks to those three operations I had last

September, I can once again fit comfortably into that little black dress that never seems to go out of style.

So it was with great anticipation that I drove to a friend's house recently for a small birthday gathering. It's really too bad that these ladies have reached that time in their lives when they can pretty much afford to have dinner anywhere in town but can't afford to put anything in their mouths. My friend had an array of mouthwatering appetizers laid out, from triple-cream Brie to a giant bowl of fresh guacamole. Everyone was standing around the room chatting politely, backed against the wall as far away from the food as possible. You'd have thought that table was contaminated with leprosy. Oh, you could see them sneaking brief, flirting glances at the food out of the corners of their eyes, but they didn't dare take a longing look lest the calories leap directly from the table into their bodies! I approached the table discreetly, fully intending to indulge in every luscious temptation on the table without making a spectacle of myself.

Our hostess had labored intensively over this exquisite feast, and I felt it was my duty not to disappoint her. Placing generous portions on a plate, I slowly worked my way around the table. I had broken the ice. Soon, others began to waver and drift in a step or two. By the time I had circled the table, the women's skirts were actually brushing the table but their backs were turned to it. I joined a conversation, nibbling from my plate between sentences. One lady's eyelashes fluttered a bit. She was obviously salivating, and she swallowed hard as I took another gulp of warm artichoke dip, trying hard not to moan in appreciation as the delicious concoction filled my mouth. I knew these ladies were suffering. One stared at me with a fixed gaze. It was barely visible, that little bit of drool from the corner of her mouth. Then she turned, faced the table, and voilà. It was a free-for-all. Forks darted under flying elbows, plates rattled, and the neatly stacked napkins exploded in a mushroom cloud. Like piranhas in a feeding frenzy, it was all

Like piranhas in a feeding frenzy,
it was all over in a few seconds!

over in a few seconds. Was I responsible for their failed discipline? Certainly not. I was simply trying to gain back the weight lost after that last surgery, I explained, unable to find a sympathetic ear in the room. Hey, a girl's gotta do what a girl's gotta do.

It was no surprise when the phone began ringing a few days later with inquiries about the possibility of chemo for weight reduction. And these women were already pros at weight loss. I was probably the only one present who hadn't been nipped, tucked, lipoed, lasered, sliced, sluiced, plumped, or prodded. (I was thinking of recommending the O.R. Guest Register for their visits to the plastic surgeon.) Most had experienced every diet pill dilemma on the market. Didn't I have just one little chemo secret I could share?

I can see the mischievous smile tickling the corners of your lips and your capitalistic brain cartwheeling into the possibilities. Move over Weight Watchers and Jenny Craig! I suppose we could handle this on a black market basis. Word travels fast in the diet underground, and business would be predictably brisk. How could I pull this off?

Let's see. I could leave some little chemo pills under pots by the front door and ask my diet customers to leave cash in the foliage. Of course, the traffic jam might alert authorities to some illegal activities, but when they see it is only middle-aged women surely they would not investigate further. Any feelings of guilt I might have would certainly wash away when I see their happy faces and trim physiques at the next neighborhood barbecue. All of my friends would be enjoying second or third helpings and enormous mountains of french fries.

No judge or jury in the land would find me guilty after the heartwarming testimonies of all the people I have helped with my chemo diet pills. When their tales of joy and satisfaction spill into the courtroom, I will be promptly and completely absolved of any crime. (If not, I could fall back on Chemo Brain and "manage" to lose my wig.)

By now I know you're wondering if I ever eat *anything* healthy or use nutritional supplements. This leads us to a very important subject.

SURVIVAL SECRET FIVE

Feed Your Body

I don't look sick even after all I've been through, and I usually joke about being chemically preserved. Maintaining good nutrition is hard work, but it's important to stay as healthy as possible. Hopefully, chemo will control the cancer, but the ravages on my body are relentless. Combine the chemo with the constant surgeries and it's war.

My regimen includes vitamins and supplements that are monitored by my osteopath, who does a battery of nutritional and digestive tests that the regular medical community doesn't; so I'm not shooting in the dark when I pop those pills and down those potions. Without that informed advice, it's a real guessing game out there.

Manufacturers try to scare you into buying their products. With sound qualified testing, however, you can make the best judgment. As you have probably noticed, there are many therapeutic options available from organizations that are eager to help us in our time of need. You're overwhelmed with information, right? In case you missed some, here are a few that caught my attention.

Pet Cures for Cancer

POSITIVE IMAGING—This is where you visualize your tumors being gone. With this kind of formidable opposition, they are supposed to just shrivel up and leave. So far my tumors and I are still in a vicious battle to see who gets to stay.

ELECTROMAGNETIC FREQUENCY—For a king's ransom, you go to Mexico and lie on a table surrounded by a halo of electronic waves. For one great price you can stay there and take these treatments for the rest of your life, or until you give up and go home (whichever comes first).

RADIO WAVES—A less expensive version of the above category. You order by mail a little box to use in the convenience of your own home. Simply plug it into any electrical outlet and hold the metal electrodes in each hand. (Not recommended for use in the bathtub.)

SOY PRODUCTS—Widely accepted as a nutritional tool in the battle to survive. If this is all you get to eat, who cares about surviving?

FERMENTED SOY PRODUCTS—Especially repugnant versions of the previous category. Although highly endorsed by alternative nutritional guru types, the gurus have never been seen actually eating any of them.

HAELAN™—If you are prepared to mortgage your home and swallow stuff that would make any grown man cry, then this particularly bilious concoction of fermented soy is for you. I call it Sewer

Sludge. Anything that tastes this bad must have an unbelievable amount of nutritional value. Promotes hair growth.

CHOCOLATE—A wonderful remedy for the products mentioned above. This necessity promotes a feeling of well-being and sublime happiness. Must be brown, warm, and gooey, preferably with nuts and caramel.

FENG SHUI—The favorable arrangement of your personal environment. My house, furniture, street, and shrubs break every rule in the book, which must be why I'm a prime candidate for cancer.

MAGNETIC ENERGY CRYSTALS—These are four crystal pyramids to be placed at the head, foot, and on each side of your bed. While you sleep, they control the flow of life-force energy, thereby promoting good health. I don't have any yet. I'm afraid that when I make my way to the bathroom, I'll fall on them in the dark.

BAMBOO SPLINTERS—This is a very effective form of mind control. When you insert these splinters under your fingernails, you no longer notice any of the side effects of chemo.

OZONE THERAPY—Readily available in Germany, the treatment involves putting ozone directly into your bloodstream, thereby eliminating all concerns about the hazards of aerosol sprays.

OZONATED OXYGEN SPA—You sit in a heated spa while ozonated oxygen is pumped in around your body. The heated spa causes exfoliation, which makes my skin delightfully soft and smooth. My tumors are not impressed but my husband is.

ESSIAC TEA—Tastes a great deal like bug extract. So far my cancer has been unresponsive, but the tea seems to work wonders for those who sell it.

GREEN TEA—Four gallons of this a day removes any need for coffee. In phase one clinical trials no one has died in the bathroom.

HERBAL TEAS—Derived from the Amazon rain forest. They turned my teeth brown just like the natives in the photographs.

BEET JUICE—At one time, I was making and drinking two quarts a day. (Warning: it leaves permanent stains on your kitchen ceiling.)

CARROT JUICE—A quart of this every day turned my hands and feet orange. My cancer cells loved the extra nutrition.

ENERGETIC BALANCING—You mail your photograph to California. A computer analyzes it, tells you how your body is malfunctioning, and prescribes some "liquid drops." They are careful not to use the word "cure." I haven't tried this remedy yet. I'm not very photogenic.

BARLEY LIFE™—Although it looks like pond scum, this green drink gives me energy. I would have trouble functioning without it. My surgeon's reports, however, all mention that my tumors continue to be "curiously green in color."

CHEMOTHERAPY—The outrageous, moderately successful practice of pumping poison directly into your veins. Fifty years from now it will be considered as barbaric as bloodletting.

Complementary therapies are both amazing and amusing because it really is a situation where "one man's trash is another man's treasure." Each individual has to find his or her own personal treasure. Try not to waste too much energy on the trash!

You feel like a truck left skid marks on your chest.

More Ways to Know You're on Chemo . . .

Your IV pole wins the downhill race at the Winter Olympics.

You practice Tibetan incantations because they're
as effective as chemo.

Your skin is so chapped that you've been elected
president of Alligators Anonymous.

You feel like a pharaoh of Egypt because you never
know what plague is coming next.

You have your teeth cleaned and your will
updated in the same week.

You resist shopping for new clothes because you
wonder if it's a bad investment.

For a change of pace, you spray paint your recliner
a different color every month.

Enchanted with the results (you're so happy to be enchanted about anything), you spray paint your head the same color.

❧

You feel like a truck left skid marks on your chest.

❧

The medical center gives you a Plaque of Honor for the most chemos that didn't work.

❧

You're so toxic you don't need a bug zapper at the outdoor barbecue.

❧

Your drug's Consumer Warning Label is twenty-three pages long, and it gives you heartburn.

❧

Life
is not a four-letter word,
but chemo is!

I paint quietly so as not to disturb him unnecessarily
as he cleans the kitchen, washes the dishes,
carries out the trash, feeds the cat,
and waters the plants.

chapter 9

The Ultimate Hobby Time Excuse

I t's time now, boys and girls, to divulge the best-kept secret of the Chemo Club. But don't let the cat out of the bag to your friends, or you and I won't be able to get an appointment. The chemo clinics will be so full they'll have to expand to every available space in the city. Civilization itself is at risk here as millions of hardworking citizens decide to go on chemo so they can have more time for their favorite hobbies. Don't pretend you don't know what I'm taking about.

Take me, for example. I was a hardworking, taxpaying, God-fearing, productive member of society ever since high school. I worked in an office for three years (too poor to go to college) and hated it. No, that's not true. I loathed it with every fiber of my young and restless soul. The airline industry offered escape and I was a flight attendant for many years. Somewhere in there I got married, had two children, and helped my husband start a business. So I was actually working three jobs simultaneously.

Hey! You're beginning to drift off there. Stay with me now, I'm getting to the point.

Art lessons had beckoned since childhood, but the opportunity just never happened. I used to stand at the kitchen sink, preparing dinner, and grit my teeth. "Take a deep breath," I'd say to myself. "Be patient. Your day will come when you can do nothing but paint." I loved my family deeply and was willing to sacrifice anything for them. It was worth it. But in my heart of hearts, I really wanted to learn to oil paint.

I managed to squeeze in a few art lessons here and there, but they only whetted my appetite. I'll swear on a stack of freshly folded laundry that I was truly born on the first day of art class when I smeared the brush around in the paint and swiped it timidly across the canvas. My breath was caught in my throat as if I had entered sacred territory. I was irreversibly addicted. I knew that painting would cause me to squander every penny, barter my children, and neglect my husband as if fleeing to an illicit lover. (Okay, so I guilt-tripped a little bit.) Every waking thought involved some scheme to carve out time to paint. In my more rational moments I realized it was an unreasonable obsession, but on another level I knew that one day this yearning would be satisfied. Chemo freed me from bondage!

I joined the ranks of the useless and unemployed and became a deliriously happy artist. Try not to snicker when I tell you that chemo was so draining, so utterly devastating to my energy level, that I was absolutely useless for anything except sitting quietly (you guessed it) at my easel, painting.

Excuse me while I drag some air into my chemo-clutched lungs and shudder pitifully. I hold onto the doorway for a moment before slowly wobbling away after the fabulous dinner prepared by my sympathetic husband. He can see that eating the dinner he slaved over for two hours has exhausted me. I must rest now and gather my strength—at the easel. I paint quietly so as not to disturb him unnecessarily as he cleans the kitchen, washes the dishes, carries out the trash, feeds the cat, and waters the plants.

Tomorrow night he'll take me out to dinner and then drop me off at my art studio so I can have some more necessary "quiet time." The restaurant experience will be draining, with all the hovering waiters, beautiful music, and rooftop view of the city at night.

"Just let me paint a while, honey, and maybe I can pull together enough energy to turn on the dishwasher tomorrow," I will offer helpfully. I refused to let him proofread this chapter. ("Oh, honey, I know how busy you are this time of year with taxes and all.") Don't any of you dare tip him off!

Getting the hang of this chemo thing, I pushed even further. My two boys were straight-A students but somehow couldn't grasp the concept of laundry management. The two knobs on the washing machine seemed more of a complex engineering marvel than the control panel of the space shuttle.

I had been a domineering, tyrannical, perfectionist mother (more guilt-tripping is in order here). Chemo got me off their backs, and they were catapulted into an intense training program in "The Care and Maintenance of Your Own Body." I promised them this would come in handy some day as I got a stool so my youngest could stand on it to reach inside the washing machine. Staggering dramatically for the proper effect, I mumbled something about throwing up. With the Hallelujah Chorus playing loudly in the background, I wobbled off to my . . .

Art Studio

In my defense, I would like to offer a sound bit of advice. Find an interest, a hobby, a passion.

99

SURVIVAL SECRET SIX

Feed Your Mind and Soul

I can be zoned out on chemo with overwhelming pain in my arms and legs, too tired to breathe, and suffering with the shakes. But if I drag myself up and go sit in front of my easel, all of that washes away. I can forget what is happening to me and the uncertainty of my life as I make the shift into the "right-brain trance." Painting is my nirvana, my meditation, my sanity, my soul. I truly do feel sorry for anyone who can only sit in a chair and suffer their aches and shakes and pain. I look at it like this—I can ache and shake in boredom *or* I can ache and shake at my easel. The choice is an easy one for me.

Everyone has to discover the source of their own nirvana. But whatever you do, don't give me any crap about being too tired! Pull yourself up by your bootstraps, turn off that garbage on TV (99 percent of television programming would bore a turnip to death), and find ways to feed your mind and soul. If you don't already know what you want, find something. Anything. Okay, so downhill racing and motorcycle jumping may be bad ideas; but heck, just the search alone will stimulate you in ways you can't imagine.

Some of you Chemo Clubbers may need more interaction with other people. My sister lives in a rural area and has been organizing efforts to improve the community center. A few months ago she too was diagnosed with cancer and at the writing of this book is undergoing chemotherapy. She and her neighbors are raising the necessary funds for the community center by serving breakfast and lunch during the week. The ladies all take turns, and my sister goes to the center three days a week to help out. Granted, she goes home to bed afterwards, but the social interaction and companionship with others is unbelievably stimulating. The ladies gab and giggle while they work and visit with all the neighbors who stop by. What a wonderful reason to get out of bed!

Excuse me? Did I hear one of you mumble something about, "What's the use?" Whoever it was please reread the preface to this book, about how happy I am that I didn't quit five years ago. Cancer is not necessarily an instant death sentence. You can enjoy the ride if you so choose.

Chemo Clubbers, arise! Go forth from your tofu-decorated sofas. Leave your recliners that are stained with spaghetti sauce and forty-five flavors of Ensure. Grab your IV poles and march defiantly out into the world!

Is it my imagination, or did you staple my incision shut
in the shape of a dollar sign?

Questions to Ask Your Doctor

When I became your patient, I had to trade down to
an economy car. Now I see you driving a new Jaguar.
Isn't that a funny coincidence?

How many more years before I can taste food again?

I forgot to put on my record that I am a medical malpractice
attorney. That's not going to be a problem, is it?

Would you consider installing a bed-and-breakfast in
your waiting room? I've been here for three days!

I've reviewed my medical bills.
I presume you'll be naming your new clinic after me?

The sign over the operating table said, "Replace Your Divots."
Are you sure that's appropriate?

The nurse said you have been practicing for many years.
Are you still just "practicing"?

Is it my imagination or did you staple my incision shut
in the shape of a dollar sign?

I have all the qualifications of a department store mannequin.
Would you give me a Letter of Recommendation for
employment?

Beyond quality
of results or success in the
marketplace, a true artist is one
who wakes up in the morning,
jumps out of bed, and shouts,
"Wow! Another day
to paint!"

Roll out the disco ball and throw on the tunes.
And hey, if the group gets a little sloppy, just
push that call button and ask for housekeeping.

chapter 10

Insurance-Approved Dinner and a Movie

"Dinner and a Movie." That's what my husband and I now call a trip to the hospital. My hospital actually has a TV and VCR in every room and a three-page list of available movies that we're working our way through. We're already on page two, column two.

I'm a little embarrassed to admit that the food at this place is great. Their desserts are world-class. If I'm in for surgery and thus denied food, I actually fantasize about the hospital's German chocolate and Italian cream cake. Consider yourself lucky if your hospital typically serves fried brake fluid patties and regurgitated seaweed. At least when they wheel you into the operating room, you're not calculating the days until your next Dutch apple crumb pie. Instead, you're free to fully concentrate on all the torture chamber devices placed strategically around the room and the strange, masked creatures moving in like characters from *Alien*. Frankly, I find it more painful to be fully cognizant of how many fabulous desserts I'm going to miss. I lie very still and gratefully slip away as the triple margarita enters the IV.

My body constantly concocts new ways to send us to the hospital. (It's no accident that I refer to my body as an entity different from myself.) In some cases, I'm just in for a few days until the doctors can figure out my latest ridiculous medical malady. My doctor and my body are like chess players calculating the next move. Since I really don't know who to cheer for, I usually just bury my face in the peach cobbler and pray there's no checkmate.

My husband and I have the drill down pat. Grab the bag and go down for "dinner and a movie." One serious mistake is to assume it's only going to be for a couple of days; that will surely get you a two-week stint. So now I happily pass on my years of experience and give you a crash course in . . .

Packing Your Hospital Bag

PILLOW—The American Medical Association and the National Institutes of Health have specific guidelines governing hospital-issue pillows. First, they must be as flat as a tongue depressor before they'll even be considered for hospital use. Further, any filling that is even remotely soft or fluffy is strictly forbidden. (I'm convinced that the recommended filling is old shredded army cots.) The most important feature of the regulation hospital pillow, of course, is its hard rubber covering. This rubber must be self-heating so as to produce a steady trickle of sweat behind the patient's ears. In scientific clinical trials conducted nationwide, it was decided that the patient's ears must turn numb within 12.467 minutes in order to produce the desired level of discomfort. In other words, your personal pillow is the first item to place in the bag.

SOCKS—I read an interesting article recently in the *American Journal of Medicine*. An industrious new intern had obviously developed a foot fetish. He actually published a paper on his findings, in which he revealed that people who occupy hospital beds have consistently cold feet. While our government rushes to fund his request for a $45,000,000,000 grant to further study this dilemma, you and I just toss a pair of socks into the bag. We've long ago discovered the immutable truth that when you've just been vivisected, your feet will be uncovered and cold for the duration of your incarceration.

GOWN—This might be the shortest topic in this book. There's been a lot of press on this subject but, Chemo Clubbers, let me ask you a question. You've just survived the Texas Chain Saw Massacre, were poured into a wheelchair, and driven off into the sunset. Do you *really* want to go home and do laundry? Their gown, they wash. Your gown, you wash. Besides, hospital gowns make you look more pathetic; therefore, your support group will bring more chocolate. No gown in the bag.

EARPLUGS—These are a must for any hospital bag. It's a well-documented fact that if you have a semiprivate room, you most assuredly will have the roommate from hell. This is nothing personal against the poor soul, but any number of the following events are guaranteed:

- ∿ Your roommate will have been admitted for treatment of an overactive bladder. Therefore, she will be continuously flushing the toilet from midnight to 5:00 AM, at which point the doctors start their rounds and finally offer medication.
- ∿ You did it. You finally get a roomie who is guaranteed to be out cold for the duration of your stay, and you'll be in complete control of the TV remote. You will quickly discover, however, that he has enough family members to populate Nebraska. Too bad his cousins never got along, and a fistfight ensues. (This actually happened!)
- ∿ Invariably you will get the scout leader whose entire troop holds its next meeting in your room. They sing all the campfire songs, practice knot-tying with your IV tubing, and show off their rappelling skills on your room divider.

- Perhaps you score a private room. Congratulations! You'll feel pretty smug, until you discover that it's across from the nurses' station and janitor's closet.
- Maybe your hospital has carpeted halls. Unfortunately, the housekeeper on your floor, striving for Employee of the Month, is forever vacuuming with a turbocharged cyclonic sweeper. I can hear your grateful voices thanking me for my years of experience. A "seasoned traveler" never leaves home without earplugs.

TOOTHBRUSH—This is your call, being so personal and all. I'm probably already in hot water with this book, having no doubt offended a gazillion people so far. I didn't want to touch the toothbrush issue but here goes. In addition to the sixteen-syllable, unpronounceable malfunction that qualified you for hospitalization, you are also guaranteed to be in imminent danger of Acute Halitosis. One of the side effects of this condition is the distinct feeling that you have just licked the bottom of the swamp with your tongue. (This is very much the same sensation you get after eating most hospital food.) Do I have to say it out loud? Take your toothbrush!

RADIO—If you succeed in driving your roommate insane so that you can have a private room, you may enjoy listening to a radio. A week's worth of daytime TV would put even a chemo brain into meltdown. Radio stations have every kind of music you could possibly want plus news, weather, and reports on all those traffic jams you're missing. In my opinion, a radio (especially one with headphones) and a good book will help ensure some degree of sanity upon dismissal.

SLIPPERS—I was at a party recently where, over a glass of wine, an architect "in the know" described the process used to chill hospital floors. No, it's not your imagination! Hospital floors really are cold and here's why: *they pump ice water through pipes under the floor in order to retard bacterial growth.* Before this process was developed, it was necessary to mop the floors with an industrial disinfectant so potent that the skin on patients' feet was peeling off! Since then, they've been able to reduce expenses by slightly diluting the mop water (and saving feet too, I imagine). But I suggest you don't even think about the fact that your floor was just "cleaned" with the same mop used on the floor in Room 47, where the unlucky fellow is being treated for stage IIIC foot fungus. Pack your slippers. Again it's only a suggestion.

HOBBY SUPPLIES—If you're in for slice and dice, you can skip this paragraph. However, if your body is as relentless as mine at tossing you in the hospital when you otherwise feel fine, hobby supplies can be a good idea. As you've gathered, I'm hard to live with when I'm not painting. I find it to be the ultimate mental distraction from the curses of chemo.

On one lengthy hospital stay, I experienced a "vertical" week and was anxious to spend it doing what I love. Oil paints are a bad idea for hospital use, but colored pencils are perfect; so my ever-obliging husband brought some of my art supplies to the hospital. I decided to start off with a small still life. Fruit seemed a likely and easy subject, so I contacted Food Services.

Just two days before, the breakfast tray had boasted two huge, beautiful strawberries. Perfect, I thought. Put those with a pear, maybe a few grapes, and I'd have exactly what I needed. I called Food Services and they were only too happy to dash some strawberries right up. What arrived was a generous bowl of . . . sliced strawberries. Trying not to look too disappointed, I thanked the girl, knowing perfectly well I had specifically ordered whole berries. That afternoon I tried one more time. Yup, sliced berries again. Surely they'd have a new crew in the kitchen tomorrow, I thought. (I knew I couldn't afford to make these people mad.)

The next day? Bingo! Big, luscious, ripe, whole strawberries that were . . . glazed! Argh. Meanwhile, the grapes I'd been hoarding were getting mighty soft. Ivy and I began calculating the maneuvers necessary for us to make it to the kitchen in person but decided it would involve too much effort. Three days later, through persistence and my bottomless charm, I finally had the necessary props. By the time I finished the painting, I had been in the hospital for nine days; so I named it Day Nine. Bad name. Who would understand?

I kept praying that my doctor would send me home, but it was not to be. I started a new painting using a rose from the bouquet a friend had sent and some more fruit. I wanted something simple so I'd be able to finish it. This one I titled, Day Fourteen, ZLUH. (ZLUH are the initials of the hospital.) Only my doctor would understand the frustration and anxiety represented in these little works of art. After I was discharged, I framed them and gave them to her. She told me how she proudly showed them off to her staff and the other doctors. Hmm. Maybe this was the wrong kind of incentive. Next time, they might keep me there longer!

Whether art or some other hobby, I strongly urge you to find something to occupy your mind and keep you busy and productive. It will make your hospital stay(s) shorter, and it's certainly better than lying there feeling sorry for yourself and dragging your family and friends down with you.

Now that we have our bag packed, we can get to other important hospital planning. Let's assume that even though you've recovered to the point of feeling okay, your insurance is continuing to pay like a rigged slot machine. Hospital administration is extremely indebted to you for your P&S (pain and suffering). The business office sends up enormous floral arrangements to show their appreciation. Big, colorful balloons decorated with dollar signs float festively over your bed. Why should we waste this party atmosphere?

Isn't your Book Review Club looking for a new meeting place, especially since Inez moved to Florida? (She served the tastiest tidbits, and her husband was always out of town.) The pantry down the hall by the nurses' station is always stocked with juice, coffee, and ice cream. It's 2:00 PM. The nurses and technicians have exhausted their list of "Creative and Bizarre New Ways to Torture Patients" and won't show up in your room again until dinnertime. I say call the group in.

Perhaps you are the Bridge Club captain. At the last meeting, things got a little boisterous. Perhaps too much wine had been served, and someone spilled their cabernet sauvignon all over Gloria's new carpet. As a result, no one wants to host now. Chemo Clubbers, there are no rules against a little wine in your hospital room. Look it up in the paperwork for yourself. As far as drinking the stuff, perhaps you're restricted by your doctor's orders, but your friends aren't. It's a rare chance for you to entertain with absolutely no obligations. This is a great opportunity to give them an afternoon to remember! Roll out the disco ball and throw on the tunes. And hey, if the group gets a little sloppy, just push that call button and ask for housekeeping.

Another opportunity that can't be ignored here involves the voluminous flowers. Because I am always on chemo and have a hard time reciprocating for all the wonderful invitations from friends, I came up with a perfect solution.

The Garden Club's hospital field trip was a serendipitous occasion! It happened during the winter months, when the only place to find an abundance of beautiful flowers is, of course, at the hospital. The various and perfect specimens had been flown in from every major flower producer in the southern hemisphere. As we visited from room to room we found everything from tulips to rare tropical blossoms, all arranged by the city's finest floral artists. Naturally, we awarded ribbons for the most impressive and unique floral arrangements. I'll bet the man in Room 33, who was zoned out on morphine after being hit by an eighteen-wheeler, was delighted when he awoke to find that the "Best of Show" ribbon had been awarded to his room. The quadruple bypass in Room 14 was thrilled to be awarded both "First Place" and "Judge's Choice." It was quite a scene as some of the other IV poles dragged their humans along for the tour. Refreshments were served, the nurses' station was presented with a beautiful arrangement, and the day was proclaimed a great success!

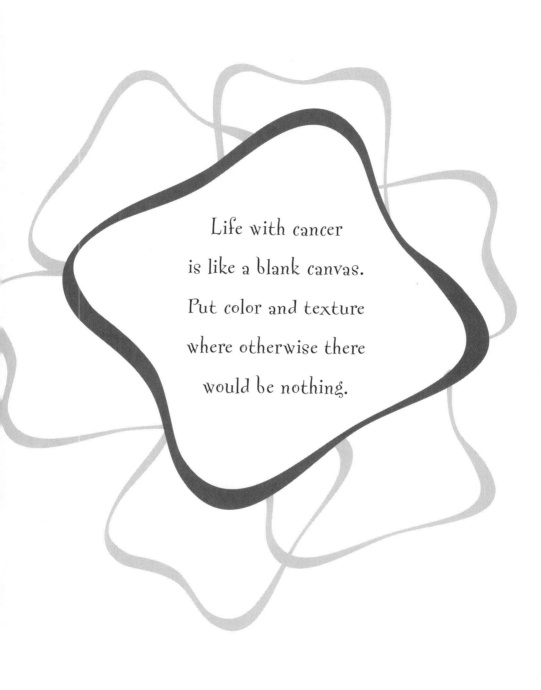

Life with cancer
is like a blank canvas.
Put color and texture
where otherwise there
would be nothing.

Tie one end of a garden hose around your
waist and the other end to a broomstick,
then practice walking around with it.

Ways to Prepare for the Ultimate Chemo Experience

Get a head start. Shave your head and buy a turban.

Tie one end of a garden hose around your waist and the other end to a broomstick, then practice walking around with it.

Fortify your immunity to discomfort by hammering your thumb.

Find recipes using tofu—or house paint.

Paint the ceilings in your house with brightly-colored designs and clever, witty musings.

Develop nerves of steel by hitching a ride on the nose of an F-14.

Convert your big, happy cookie jar into a pill repository.

Buy a medical dictionary so you can cross-examine your
doctor and impress your friends with such words as
phosphatidylserine and *ileosigmoid reanastomoses.*

⚜

Roll naked in poison ivy so you can practice being jolly
while experiencing a full body rash.

⚜

Decorate your lap blanket with all your friends'
numbers so you don't have to crawl to the kitchen
for your address book.

⚜

Tie yourself to the bottom of a cliff and set off an avalanche.

⚜

Convert every chair in your house to a recliner.

⚜

Take your brain out and hang it up to dry.

The
Art of Life

Steps
Of
Survival

Steps of Survival

O kay, Chemo Clubbers, up until now we've been having a lot of fun, and some of you may be asking, "Where's the beef?" You were supposed to be reading between the lines as we gaily explored the chemo lifestyle, but I suspect that some of you haven't been taking me seriously. Now it's time to do our homework.

You will not be distracted in this chapter by whimsical cartoons, flights of fantasy, or meddling editors polishing my sentences in an effort to make me look respectable. I looked cancer in the face a long time ago and declared war. "The Art of Life" is my personal game plan with the minute-to-minute, day-by-day structure I have followed for quality of life and survival. This is what I call the "hard-core how-to."

From my heart to yours, here it is, delivered straight up and uncut.

ESTABLISH A CORPORATION

Separate your brain from your body. No, this is not the Texas Chain Saw Massacre; this is executive leadership. Question: How is it possible that a Chief Executive Officer can successfully manage a world-class corporation through a myriad of challenges, but cannot manage his/her own body when faced with a health crisis?

Think of the body as a corporation composed of a multitude of departments, each with various and diverse duties, all working together for profit and productivity. Every successful corporation needs leadership: a CEO. Your brain is your CEO, and your body is the corporation that you were given to work with. Like any good CEO, you must put objectivity over emotionalism, and maximize your potential. Your brain must be able to observe the problems, assess the solutions, and manage your corporation with logic, common sense, and leadership. As the CEO of your corporation, you must sometimes make difficult, unpopular decisions for the good of the whole. Like a parent managing a child, your head must remain above the fray.

Nothing ever quite prepares you for managing a life with cancer. Staying alive is a full-time job. The medical community has an infuriating habit of talking to you about "buying time," and "quality of life." You silently scream, "But I'm too young! I want more."

Listen to me. I'll tell you how to have more. The answer lies in your brain. With mental determination, mental discipline, mental focus, and a little mental distraction—you *can* attain the reward known as "quality of life," and have joy.

Put your brain in control of your corporation. It's good for business!

BREATHE!!

Huh? How dumb do we think you are that you have to be reminded to breathe? Wait a minute! Hear me out on this. Deep breathing exercises are so important, they go at the top of the SOS list.

Conscious effort is required here, so pay attention. The process starts before you get out of bed in the morning, and continues regularly throughout the day. Ideally, at least every two hours, follow these steps:

1. Straighten your spine and, if possible, sit up.

2. Pull air into your lungs slowly, hold for a count of ten, and let it out slowly.

3. Repeat this ten times, each time trying to feel the air "hit bottom" in your lungs.

Whoa! We don't want you to hyperventilate, so remember to take slow, deep breaths.

Why is breathing so important? Among other things, it helps clear the brain. Chemo seems to close up the lungs, and if you aren't providing oxygen to your blood stream, you will find it hard to get energy. I do breathing exercises before and after eating or exercise, and hourly throughout the day.

Breathing is good for business. If you make breathing an automatic part of your SOS, then you'll be able to accomplish the other ambitious steps on this list!

GET OUT OF BED

Most of us know the Bible story about Jesus who was martyred on the cross, laid to rest, and on the third day rose again. Our religious leaders teach us how and why this is important, and the lessons for mankind. Those of us in the Chemo Club know that there is *another* lesson in this story: folks, if you've been lying there for three days, *IT'S TIME TO GET UP!*

Staying too long in bed has many crippling side effects; your muscles turn to jelly, your digestive system gets lazy, and you have trouble processing and eliminating food so you get constipated. You probably are not getting the proper nutrition, and most likely not getting enough fluids. Your CEO knows that every department in your corporation is, forgive the pun, *lying down on the job,* and gets depressed, so leadership fails. In other words, you will bankrupt your corporation!

Most things in life have a methodical process, and getting out of bed happens to be one of them.

1. Start with the deep-breathing exercises explained earlier.

2. Try to stretch every moving part, starting with the small ones (fingers and toes), and moving up to the larger ones.

3. Massage your scalp.

4. Visualize your activities. Did you ever notice how the Olympic high diver stands poised on the end of the board, and mentally goes through the motions required to execute a perfect dive? Who knew that one day you would need this kind of mental concentration just to *get out of bed?*

5. Read something funny.

You think I'm joking, don't you? If you think this is insipid drivel, let me tell you that I know your physical and emotional pain. I know where you hurt and how badly you hurt, except for the places that are completely numb! I also know what works when you're zoned out on chemo and/or pain medication, and that if you just lie there, your brain focuses on your pain, and you easily become depressed. If you get up and move around, you give your brain something else to think about. The hardest thing I do every day is get out of bed, using the very steps outlined above. And because I do it, I've been able to produce beautiful paintings, meet with galleries and clients, laugh with friends, and have *quality of life*. Getting out of bed makes good business sense.

LAUGHTER

Since I'm afraid we still have some sour-faced skeptics in the group, I'm going to risk annoying you, and visit this issue again. Let's get down to the basics. In the beginning, God created the heaven and earth. He made birds to swim in the ocean and fish to fly in the sky. *(Gotcha!)* Just wanted to see if you are paying attention. Now that I think you're not just looking at these words, we'll continue. He made all kinds of animals and creatures to inhabit this earth, including man and woman. Some people believe what separates human beings from the rest of the creatures is our soul. We don't really know if animals have souls, but it does make us feel superior. There is one undeniable fact, however: the singular asset that defines mankind as a higher life-form is the ability to laugh. We have all been empowered with the gift of mirth and the strength to laugh. But it's up to you to use it.

In the battle to survive and enjoy *quality of life*, you have already noticed that some of the things you once did for fun and pleasure have suddenly become medicine. Laughter is in that category. I don't mean just a smile or momentary amusement. I am speaking of knee-slapping, gut-wrenching, floor-rolling LAUGH-TER. You know where to find it; it's all around you. Books, comedy tapes, movies, friends, etc. As I explained earlier, one of my greatest allies against depression and fatigue is the steady stream of funny jokes off the Internet that a dear friend faxes to me every few days. Does this sound ridiculously simple? Yes. Does it *work?* YES! When I catch myself overly fatigued, melancholy, or losing intestinal fortitude, I open my mind and seek humor with "mirthful intent." In other words, I give myself "permission to play." I'll be honest; sometimes it takes three days of funny movies or tapes to get my head on straight, and bring myself into balance.

Constant vigilance is required. Along with the search for humor, an equal effort should be made to reject drama and trauma. In other words, don't read the front page of the newspaper; you'll still be well informed if you want to be, but it always puts sand in your teeth and makes you wonder what's worth living for. Avoid TV programs and movies that contain violence, heartbreak, drama, and trauma. Your life is already full of heartbreak, drama, and trauma; why would you want to involve your energy and emotions in something concocted by Hollywood? You know what food to put on your plate, so understand what food to put in your brain. You wouldn't let a child watch porn or vicious scenes (hopefully) because you know it's not good for them. By the same token, *know* what's good for *you.* If I want to get out of bed or pull up my bootstraps, I pick up the stack of humor and start reading. The laughter always energizes me and clears my brain.

Laughter gives energy; tears drain energy. Laughter makes you strong; tears make you weak. Laughter will give you zest and enthusiasm for life, which are so critical for survival. Work as hard on mental attitude as you do on nutrition. Constantly nourish your body, and relentlessly avoid anything that is not uplifting.

Try it. This is neither naïveté nor denial; this is skillful mental distraction, and it's good for business!

EXERCISE

To help you get out of bed, do some stretches. (Remember, you've already done your breathing, so the next step is to convince your body to actually move.) Some days I feel like the most strenuous exercise I can manage is to lift my left eyelid; for some reason, the right eyelid is more cooperative. But we *must push farther*. Yes, I know you feel like mincemeat; stop whining. It's important to help your body maintain some strength. If you're accustomed to a lethargic lifestyle, start with simple yoga stretches lying down.

In yoga, try to hold each position about two minutes, concentrating all your thoughts on methodical breathing, and "letting go" of your tense muscles, so you can relax into the pose. It is only natural for you to become distracted and let your mind wander. You visualize calling 911 and requesting the JAWS OF LIFE to remove you from this position. You fantasize about installing a First Alert System so you can cry out, "Help! I'm stuck in the Lotus Position and can't get up!" You worry about being the subject of the evening news: "Chemo Clubber rescued after five days in the Reclining Hero Pose."

If these thoughts are creeping in, it's your signal that you must practice mental focus. Besides, it's hard to perform good yoga while you're giggling. Return to your breathing and muscle control. If you're visualizing your activities for the day, and what you want to accomplish, this is permitted. After all, who doesn't dream of grocery shopping?

Cardio workout, even a reclining bicycle, is fantastic stimulation for mind and body. You don't need a "health club" for exercise. You can move around your room, hall, or yard. You can do "step" exercises or jog in place. Hold a can of peaches in each hand and do weight lifting. Put that same can in a long sock and tie it around your ankle for leg lifts. Put all your medical bills in a box and "bench press" them. (Try to resist the urge to "shot put" them out the window.) Exercise that brain muscle and use your imagination, for goodness sake.

At the expense of using more ink, I'll tell you what works for me. When I'm on the treadmill, I concentrate on the rhythm of motion and my arms. When that fails to do the trick, I concentrate on feeling the movement in my stomach and thighs. As my body begins to complain and rebel, I focus on pushing my knees forward, and then picking up my heels. This is where the mental determination and mental discipline begin. You're out of excuses. Try to maintain a steady program and build your endurance. It's good for business!

S. A. D.
Stress, Anger, Depression

Interesting, isn't it, when you lump these things together, and the result is overwhelming grief? Like cancerous tumors, they are hopelessly intertwined, and self-feeding. Any one factor alone immediately results in the complete package. But like that proverbial bundle of sticks, if you attack them individually and start managing each part, the bundle disappears.

A key to stress management is definition: is it a problem, a nuisance, or a minor inconvenience? The whole concept of stress is a product of our times. This is the age of victimization, self-indulgence, and lack of personal responsibility. Stress is an excuse for us to be weak and lay the blame on something or someone "beyond our control." Our senses are constantly assaulted by the noisy, the angry, the destructive; and we *allow* it to happen. We are confronted in every aspect of our lives, sometimes in our families, and even in our entertainment. You have enough real challenges in normal everyday life without adding unnecessary factors. Try to examine your daily activities, and remove things that cause you stress. For instance, too much in our environment blasts you with a loud cacophony of sounds designed to get your attention and raise your blood pressure. Masquerading as energy and pleasure, this is stress in its simplest form. Disharmony in any form is stress. If you can't hit the "off" button, then remove yourself.

Let's say the cable man has been crawling around in your attic, dislodges the condensate line from the air conditioner, and doesn't tell you. Three days later you open a bedroom door, the ceiling is lying on the carpet, and everything is water-damaged (this actually happened to me). Stress, and *not your fault!* But how do you respond? It's not life threatening, and it will still be there after your nap. Learn to acknowledge what is causing you stress. Put every-thing into perspective. "If it weren't for stress, I'd have no energy at all." If stress is your friend, then use it—or lose it. If it's causing you *anger and depression,* put your CEO in charge and control it. Before you dismiss this as naïve simplicity, understand that you walk a thin and fragile line, and you need every nerve and fiber devoted to maintaining a healthy mental attitude. This is hard-core survival at its finest!

Anger. Ah, yes. There are *so many* reasons to be angry. "Anger is like acid. It does more damage to the vessel in which it is stored, than that onto which it is poured." Maybe anger is keeping you alive, or maybe it's destroying your energy reserves and causing you *stress and depression.* Even the young and healthy will find their paths are growing shorter and narrower. Do you *really* want to spend your remaining days devoted to anger? At least be clever and creative about it, and use anger to your advantage, which could be good mental distraction. If someone has done you a great injustice, then promise to send them your spleen. In other words, live it and love it . . . or let it go!

Depression is like cancer: left to grow and fester, it will destroy your body. Also like cancer, it is often difficult to recognize, and sometimes the symptoms are vague and indefinable. Depression: *tears in the brain = tears in the heart = tears in the body*. Learn to recognize tears in the brain, because a sick mind cannot help a sick body. Stress and anger will inevitably bring you to depression, and once there, the danger is that you *just may not care anymore*. To put it bluntly, you will bankrupt your corporation! Depression takes away your life, and laughter gives your life back to you.

GIVE TO OTHERS

Not your money—that's too easy. Not your gallbladder—you don't need it anyway.

Give your most precious assets: your time and your knowledge.

This doesn't necessarily mean shoveling potatoes at the local soup kitchen. Those folks are the most hardened survivors on the face of the earth! (Maybe they could teach you a thing or two.)

Listen to others' needs; give of yourself and your intelligence. Even if you are only seven years old, you have knowledge that someone else could use. You have value.

When another artist comes to me for advice, instruction, ideas, or critique, I am only too happy to help. I receive calls regularly from someone wanting advice on handling a life with cancer. Whether my solutions work for them is of no consequence. What matters is that I tried, and I shared.

Recognize the benefits for YOU: sharing provides an outlet,

companionship, mental stimulation, and mental distraction. It's good for business!

FOLLOW YOUR DREAM

Perhaps you're tired of hearing me beat this drum, but this is where we give that overworked CEO a break. Every great leader needs "time out," and this survival step is so drastically important, it demands its own category.

When I talk about pursuing your dream, I'm not suggesting your look up your old high school sweetheart, I'm talking about your ultimate mental distraction. What can you use to give you the incentive to get up every day, to keep going against impossible odds, to keep you putting one foot in front of the other and give you quality of life? What is it that fills your soul, and will provide the ultimate mental distraction? That is what we need now, to divert our focus from our pain and the uncertainty of our lives, and place that focus on something positive and personally fulfilling. Miles Davis, the great musician, once said during an interview that the music was always in his head, no matter what activity he was engaged in at the moment, even sleeping. I knew instantly what he meant, because as an artist, I am always painting in my head, whether I'm at my easel or not. I have used this mental distraction and mental focus as a valuable tool to help me through the darkest hours. When the chemo is causing me overwhelming pain and I have the shakes, if I am distracted by my oil painting, all of that washes away. I forget about everything, and the hours pass quickly by. Getting up out of the chair, or out of bed, and getting started is the hardest part. Sometimes I actually have to visualize myself standing up and going through the motions. Mental determination gets you up, so that mental distraction can take over. In the terrifying days before surgery, when my mind is having trouble focusing an *anything*, I take refuge in my painting.

Because I make this effort, my life is filled with the beauty I have created, admiring collectors, clients who commission me to fill a special request, exciting possibilities, and joy. Is it hard work? Of course, but the rewards literally keep me breathing!

Would've, could've, should've. The world is full of them, but it's never too late to get started. Everyone has something that intrigues them, which they find entertaining and fulfilling. Maybe you haven't really latched onto yours yet, or maybe it has just been tucked away dormant in the back of your mind, lost among the cobwebs. Recently someone remarked that he was envious of my art, and wished he had *something* similar in his life. I asked whether he ever had a dream about a particular interest, and he replied, "Yes, I always wanted to do storytelling." I asked him if he had done anything lately about pursuing his dream, and the reply was, "No." Then I asked, "Every night after you come home and have dinner, do you watch television until bedtime?" "Yes, I'm tired." So I said to him, "Do you realize that is four hours—literally a half day of valuable time—that you *could* be involved in learning about or doing storytelling? And do you realize that if you were involved in storytelling, your tiredness would wash away, and you would find yourself surprised to be up so late?" A few weeks later I saw a notice in the paper that a Storyteller's Convention would be held in our city and sent it to him. Did he go, or is he still just wishing?

I know a cancer patient who loves gardening; her yard overflows with colorful flowers, her figs are as big as pears, and her pears look like pineapples! This is her therapeutic mental distraction, and her beautiful, bountiful rewards are obvious. All of her friends get to share in the glory, and their happiness gives her a double return on her investment. Last December, an acquaintance reported that apathy, lethargy, and depression (the "killer trio") had settled in on our gardener. I suggested that since the weather had changed, she needed to find a way to get involved in her gardening through the winter months. She did, and it worked! It's not that I'm so smart, or have answers to everyone's problems; it was just common sense. Many people find that helping out in their community is very rewarding, and has the added bonus of companionship and interaction with others. These social contacts could be your greatest supporters!

Wait a minute! Did someone just say, "Why bother?" Cancer is not necessarily an instant death sentence. You may look back years from now, and chastise yourself for wasting so much time. You probably have a lot of time on your hands, and if you think about it, chemo is the greatest hobby excuse there is. We all know you're pretty useless for anything except pursuing your favorite pastime! There just aren't many valid excuses for you to deny yourself this reward. If you haven't found your passion, keep looking. The search will occupy your CEO and provide some much-needed distraction. Okay, so rock climbing may be a shaky idea right now, but I promise there is a place for you somewhere, even in connection with this activity. Go ahead and lay some groundwork for the future. No matter what your handicaps or limitations, something is waiting to fill that void in your life. We even hear of paraplegics who hold the pencil in their teeth to create beautiful drawings. Don't you feel a little ashamed to be so lazy? Pursuing your dream could be your greatest weapon against depression and IT'S GOOD FOR BUSINESS!

THE WORLD WILL FOLLOW YOUR LEAD

Living with cancer and chemotherapy requires excellent corporate teamwork. One of the most vital things your CEO can do is to manage your environment, including those around you. If you want to get the most from your support team, then you need to give them the best possible attitude to work with. In other words, *take care of your caregiver!* It is extremely important *for your own good* that your family, friends, and caregiver be of spirit and good humor. If you are always down in the dumps and focused on your mutilated body, they will be too. If you moan endlessly about all the gory details and how bad you hurt, your team may have a hard time giving you the kind of atmosphere and support you need. This does not mean that you ignore pain or pretend you don't have cancer; when I openly and matter-of-factly discuss it, people are more at ease and relaxed in my company. In the beginning, you may find that people are uncomfortable and don't know how to react around you, so it is important for you to set the tone. No one wants to be around a morbid grump!

Let's face it folks: we need our friends and family desperately. They are the glue that holds us together. They manage our world so that we can manage our illness. Their workload doubles as ours diminishes. We are permitted to collapse, phase out, whine, and soak up all the sympathy, while they have to be strong and stoic. They can see how you struggle, they love you and want to help you in every way possible, but they are only human. They have worries, aches, and problems, *plus* the anguish of seeing you suffer. What we absolutely cannot have is our support team falling apart on us. May I speak frankly? You need your team to be standing up, helping, *and happy!* It's in your best interest to be a leader with spirit, good humor, and sportsmanship. They will be so grateful, you'll be rewarded with LOTS of chocolate! Is this devious manipulation? Absolutely! But no one will accuse you of being a chemo scam artist. You need to be strong, patient, and resourceful. Managing cancer is a big job, and you have to pull it out of your guts, or a cast of thousands can't help you.

An amazing transformation happens when we take charge of the situation and decide to manage our illness with spirit and good humor: everyone around us acts and feels better, so *we* feel better. If we laugh, we will hear laughter. This is definitely good for business! Like looking into a mirror, the world will reflect your image. Is this naïveté or denial? No. This is executive leadership at its finest!

NUTRITION

Yeah, yeah, yeah; you've heard it ad nauseum. Too many of you naughty Chemo Clubbers aren't even putting enough fluids or food in the gas tank. You used to eat and drink for fun, but now it's medicine for survival, and you're no longer interested. Oh, cruel irony! This is a really big challenge for your CEO, and demands some of that mental discipline we were talking about earlier. Do you see that decrepit plant over by the window that looks like its been on chemo for years? Take heed: without food and water, *your petals are going to droop.*

But we're not talking tofu here. Everything you ever needed to know about good nutrition, you learned in third grade, and I'm going to forget about all of your past sins. Now you're suddenly concerned about good nutrition, and self-flagellating over fried chicken. Most of you have already noticed that chemo or radiation has put a serious dent in your normal eating habits, and your "bloomin' onion" days are over! You're suddenly reading up on vitamins and antioxidants, and mail-ordering all sorts of exotic stuff you can't pronounce. Every magazine that somehow finds its way to your kitchen table is cover-to-cover anxiety, and all sorts of concerned organizations are ready to stock your pantry with the next miracle. Feeling a little overwhelmed, you say?

How do you know if all of this stuff is actually doing you any good? How do you know what your body really needs and what it's lacking? How many of these products are overlapping, and where are the gaps? Is your body actually absorbing anything you swallow, or is it simply eliminating the deluge? In addition to the complete nutrition panel you should request in every blood test, there are osteopaths who order tests to analyze your nutritional and mineral needs, and digestive functions. With sound, qualified testing, you can put your time and money where it does the most good.

If there's wheatgrass growing in your garage and you're taking the herbal route, realize that these things take time. Realistically, it can take three to six months for your body to respond. Educate yourself about all of the drugs and complementary remedies you are consuming. Watch closely for allergies or contraindications, to be sure you are not defeating your own purposes. Tell your doctor about all of the nutritional supplements you are consuming, because it's important for the left hand to know what the right hand is doing. Your doctor may actually know something about complementary nutritional supplements, and have warnings or suggestions. If your doctor shrugs and snickers at you, consider "changing quarterbacks."

While we're visiting alien territory, let's talk about alternative therapies for cancer that can take you to foreign and exotic places. Let common sense and logic rule. If it sounds like voodoo, it probably is voodoo. You may have already discovered an alternative therapy that costs a king's ransom, and the clinic-provider can't give you references due to "protecting its clients' privacy." Question: if this treatment cured *your* cancer, wouldn't you want the world to know and gladly shout it from the rooftops so you could save others from suffering? So much for the privacy issue. However, you may hear from a patient of one of these clinics, who is intensely anxious for you to dash immediately to the treatment center. Further investigation may reveal that this person is also a "patient coordinator," and has an economic interest in your health.

We all need to have hope, and sometimes we are truly desperate to take risks for the slimmest chance of survival. Just ask yourself and your doctor one basic question: "Is there any shred of sound logic in the protocol of this treatment?"

Now go drink another glass of water, and choke down some beet juice.

FRIENDS AND THE WHINE LINE

As you've hopefully already discovered, friends can be your staunchest supporters in the quest for that vague and indefinable state known as "quality of life." Like a box of chocolates, each friend has a certain flavor and fills a certain corner of your life. But in order to have a friend, you must *be* a friend. Just because you are faced with character-building challenges doesn't mean you are allowed to only take. You must also give. Remember that your friends also have aches, concerns, and problems, and sometimes they can be overwhelmed. When friends call to inquire about your current condition, give them the "fine-fine" response, and if they push for more, give them an abbreviated update. (You can't really crush them with the agony; it will overload their systems, and then they may resist the next encounter. Save it for the Whine Line.) Then, as quickly as possible, move the conversation to what is happening in *their* lives. You will find it mentally distracting from your own problems, and entertaining to hear an update on what is going on with them. Occasionally, you must initiate the call because they are very busy and may be afraid to disturb you, or to hear bad news. One friend named Robbin is very busy with her family and a corporate career, plus she is required to travel a lot. Sometimes I call and tell her I need a "Robbin fix;" we catch up on each other's news and have some laughs. You are not the only one who likes to know they are missed. Your friends have waited during your surgeries, stood by your hospital bed, showered you with home-cooked goodies, and made you feel loved and needed. Your acts of friendship don't have to be grand, glorious, or expensive. Often, the simplest overtures will be the most appreciated: clipping out a funny cartoon that reminds you of their situation, with a follow-up phone call, can earn you lots of laughs and goodwill.

And now about the Whine Line. Here is some inside information you won't hear from anyone else. For a certain friend who sometimes experiences health problems or an especially stressful situation that they just need to get off their chest, we have the Whine Line. Everyone needs a place to "unload" now and then. When a phone call is made, the response is, "The Whine Line is now open." We take turns moaning and complaining about all of our problems, fears, or concerns, knowing everything will be held in absolute confidence. We listen intently and make suggestions to each other. Then we have a big laugh, tell a couple of jokes, and promise that we are always available for the Whine Line. This has been a very valuable asset in handling my medical challenges, and taking some of the burden off my family.

One more thing about friends: please do yourself a favor, and take every opportunity to accept invitations to join them for a meal or get-together. Hush, it's *me* you're talking to. I know your head is swimming, your body feels like it was hit by a train, your hands, feet, and mouth are numb, you have a complete body rash, and your skin is peeling off. You may even still be a little stiff from that last surgery. Sorry—not valid excuses to stay home. They won't care if you show up in your sock feet because you can't tolerate shoes. Put a bauble on your toe and call yourself "Little Egypt." Drag your carcass up, throw on your camouflage gear, and join them. I *promise* that for a little while the fog will clear, you'll enjoy the conversation and laughs, and you'll be showered with hugs and compliments about how *good you look* (the camouflage gear is great, huh?). Tip: you're there for the laughs, not group therapy. Don't talk about cancer or chemo, and NEVER talk about your pains. The outing will be uplifting, and for days you'll bask in the warm glow of the memories.

P.S. You probably thought you were through with me, but there is just one more thing: I strongly encourage you to actively cultivate new friends. Each of us knows at least a hundred people whom we've thought would be really interesting or fun to visit with and get to know better. What are you waiting for? Take the time, *make the time*, to get to know them. Don't wait for them to initiate the invitation; you have a phone, so pick it up and put a date on your calendar. Don't even mention cancer unless they do, and keep it brief. You're there for entertainment and to forget about it for a little while. Another promise: you will find it unbelievably stimulating and rewarding. Trust me, it's good for business.

PAIN MANAGEMENT
Drugs versus Discipline

Sorry, Chemo Clubbers, but this is where the rubber meets the road, and we find out what we're made of. One way to approach this problem is to ask yourself if this pain is a problem, or an inconvenience. Kind of like when you take your car back to the dealership for the tenth time, finally realize it's not going to get any better, and decide to live with it. If you're over fifty, you've already negotiated an agreement with pain, because you can't remember the last time you got out of bed and didn't hurt somewhere.

Everyone has a level at which pain is intolerable, more commonly known as a "pain threshold." The medical community has a pain measurement scale invented by a twenty-five-year-old mechanical engineer in the late 1600s. Your doctor will hand you a form to fill out with questions like, "On a scale of one to ten, how bad is this pain?" You try to remain calm as you visualize inserting this form, pencil, and clipboard into the left nostril of your medical technician. However, you are now an experienced member of the Chemo Club and have perfected the art of self-control. You gently explain that you aborted your dream vacation in Tahiti on which you spent your life savings and arrived via Medi-Jet because your pain is ONE THOUSAND, SIX HUNDRED AND THIRTY-FIVE!! So if he would please hand you the morphine button immediately, you promise not to remove his Adam's apple with your fingernails. Remember to smile endearingly.

I have a personal pain measurement scale, which you are welcome to use if you wish: does this hurt more or less than smashing my hand in a car door? All joking aside, you are not expected to suffer needlessly, and there will be times when you must have medication. Unfortunately, most pain medication works by numbing the brain, which completely ruins your life. You remain in a foggy stupor. If this suits your purpose, then enjoy it. However, if you want to remain functional on a certain level, then ask your doctor if there is a different medication you can use for pain that does not turn you into a zombie. You may have to negotiate a little with your "pain threshold," but at least you'll get to have a life. You won't be surprised to learn that I use laughter, art (my passion), mental distraction, and mental discipline to keep pain medication to an absolute minimum. After surgery, I wean myself off pain medication as quickly as possible. Yeah, it hurts; so what else is new? I have things to do.

One more thing: permission to sleep. If you have problems getting a good night's sleep, ask for a sleep aid. This is different from a sleeping pill. The chemo drugs and steroids that accompany them can prevent you from sleeping at night, and it is critical that you get good rest. When you get up in the morning, you're better able to make the most of your day. (More of that "quality of life" stuff.)

KNOW YOUR BODY

As CEO of your corporation, understand that if you're not paying attention, no one is. You know every ping and rattle in your auto, but do you know your body? If you're undergoing treatment, keep a chart for a month or two and look for patterns to develop. This will allow you to make plans for the "good days" so you can do that "quality of life" thing. Pay attention to changes, no matter how trivial they may seem. We don't suggest hypochondria or paranoia, but it is important to check things out before a situation is out of control. Sometimes the cancer treatments trigger strange responses in the body that are seemingly unconnected to the treatment. A symptom may seem like a chemo side effect but could actually be another condition that needs to be treated. Especially if you are new to the Chemo Club, many side effects and bodily responses occur that you are not aware of, so check them out! Using common sense and logic is always a good idea. Try to qualify what you are experiencing: Is it because of something you did or did not do? Could it be a reaction to some medication, or it is because people in your age group commonly experience the same symptom(s)? When the body is out of balance, you suffer needlessly. A blood test can indicate you need more fluids, medication for red or white cells, nutrition, or some other malfunction that could be easily remedied. Even though your tests were fine just a few days ago, sometimes your condition can change rapidly, so don't hesitate to call your doctor. If your nausea is not being controlled, tell your doctor. A change in medication could help, because the same medication doesn't always work for everyone. Don't worry about "bothering" your doctor; if you don't let doctors know, how can they help you?

Stay informed. Read your radiologist's report, follow your blood tests, and if you are enchanted by Frankenstein movies, read your surgeon's operative reports. When you are meeting with your doctor to review the latest test, ask for a copy right then and there, because coaxing it from Medical Records later will be more challenging than chemo. Keep good medical records because you never know when you might want to change teams, and you'll be ready. If you have drug allergies, read the fine print and watch for contraindications. When you pick up a prescription from the pharmacist, review the Patient Information advisory and try not to have a heart attack when you read the list of "possible side effects." Ask for product information on every drug you are given, especially if you are prone to allergic reaction. Hey, no one ever said this would be easy; staying alive is a full-time job. Remember: *you're in charge.*

WORSHIPPING YOUR FAITH

We are going out on a limb here, and may be stepping on some toes. We already know that managing cancer is a tricky business, full of risks and potholes. So with reckless abandon, I am going to ask you a difficult question. When you go to your place of worship, does it fill you with joy, comfort, and contentment? Or do you return home feeling a little melancholy and blue? Is the rest of the day spent on the sofa in a lethargic state of near-depression? Hey, maybe you work hard all week, and this is your day to be a couch potato, watch a movie, or see your favorite team get slaughtered on TV. Just asking, that's all.

The nature of humanity is preordained to need and believe in a "higher power." Most religions focus on two important facets: rules to live by in this life and looking forward to the afterlife. This is a necessary and rewarding part of living and should not be taken lightly. When you are managing a life crisis such as cancer, however, you must examine every aspect of your activities to guard against that "D" word, depression. Does your faith remind you a little too much about that "afterlife"? Are you surprised to find yourself a little reluctant about the possibility of reaching that crossroad? Is it possible to maintain the zest and enthusiasm necessary for survival, and at the same time, joyfully anticipate the afterlife? Just asking.

If you find that attending worship services and hearing music that reminds you of funerals is just a little depressing, consider finding another way to practice your faith. Religion is so extremely personal it is something in your soul that can be practiced in an intensely private manner. Every house of worship has a full agenda of activities in which you can become involved to practice and exemplify your faith. You may have already found that this social interaction is great therapy for you. If you haven't looked for solutions there, maybe you should consider doing so. If you have limited access to transportation, houses of worship can often make arrangements for you.

Sometimes people who have not been previously active in a religion find new peace and comfort if they add this to their life. You can even start out slowly, attending social functions and activities designed to be supportive and uplifting.

Examine your personal circumstances, and figure out what is right for you. Someone else's solutions might not work for you. The main idea is to consider lifestyle changes that could improve your attitude management.

SELECTING YOUR DREAM TEAM

It is imperative that you are comfortable with your doctors, and have faith in their ability to oversee your medical care. Your CEO has a really big job keeping your corporation running smoothly, and shouldn't have to be worrying about the treatment you are receiving. We don't like to hear bad news, and it is good to get second opinions. If your doctor is a true professional, he or she will not be insulted if you seek another opinion; in fact, that is expected. When it comes to cancer treatment, you will probably find that the "first-line therapy" is the same all over the country. The first line of attack is the most tried and true, with the greatest success rate. Even the second- and third-line therapies often follow proven paths. It's when you get farther down the road, and your cancer persists, that sometimes your doctors have to be creative. I call it "power thinking in the shower." Cancer seems to be individually specific, and the drugs that are successful for one person may be ineffective for another. You need to be aware of your options and of the risks involved. Some cancer clinics follow a certain protocol of treatment, and your doctor may be controlled by the requirements of his institution. Don't hesitate to visit a different institution in your effort to find answers that may work for you. Once you've changed doctors, always consider it an option to return to your original team. Don't be handicapped by your own sensitivities in your quest for life.

Make sure your doctor is paying attention when you discuss your symptoms and concerns. Sometimes doctors are overloaded and don't *really listen.* I once had a doctor who was highly recommended and admired in his field. I respected his judgment immensely, and was very confident of his ability. When I visited his office, however, he couldn't put *both* feet in the room. He literally stood straddling the threshold, ready to bolt down the hall to the next patient. I actually insisted at one point that he come into the room and sit down! You'll notice that I speak of this doctor in the past tense. If your game plan is failing, don't be afraid to change quarterbacks.

When you go to meet with your doctor, have questions and problems *written down.* Trust me when I say that you probably won't remember everything while you're there. Make a list; tape a piece of paper on your bathroom mirror, and as you prepare for bed every night, write down any questions, complications, or problems you've had. Be sure to take this list with you when you visit your doctor. Your doctor will respect you for being prepared, and your meeting time will be used efficiently. We're not all going to win this battle, but it is very important that you feel you are getting the best treatment that is medically and scientifically possible.

FATIGUE

By now you've probably got it figured out. If you've been following the previous steps and reading between the lines, you may have already noticed that the answer to fatigue is all of the steps outlined on the previous pages. There is a pattern in these Steps of Survival that I refer to as the "M Strategy": methodical, manipulative, mental management. Every page in this chapter presents a guide for you to manage the facets of your life with clear, common sense and logical focus. If you make each of these steps an automatic part of every day, fatigue should become less of an issue. Of course, your blood tests will reveal if you need medication to boost your blood count, but there is always a gap in there between normalcy, and what qualifies you for medication. That gap is where your CEO must take control with focus and management.

Every one of these steps is designed to involve your brain in actively focusing on a particular task. When you give your mind a clear, positive duty on which to focus, you spend less time dwelling on pain and unhappiness. If you think about it, there's not much here that is earth-shattering revelation. It is just common sense, but amazingly, many people don't do this simple self-management. When facing a health crisis, their brains are so overloaded with pain and anxiety, they are consumed by chaos and can't think straight. This is a natural reaction, but it will bankrupt your corporation! Put order in your life with clear, concentrated, logical purpose. Never take your eyes off the prize: life. I named this chapter "The Art of Life" because it provides an outline that applies to anyone in normal everyday living, whether they are young or old, healthy or facing a challenge.

When fatigue is overwhelming you, how can I make you understand that getting a little exercise will slowly help you improve? You must take control of your life and go forward with determination and purpose. Managing cancer, chemotherapy, and all of the other treatments is a full-time job. Sometimes it is very difficult to keep going hour by hour, day by day, week after month after year, and some of us know there is no light at the end of the tunnel. But it is *possible* to have it all: a disease *and a life!* Becoming discouraged is dangerous and deadly (more "D" words). This is why you need a game plan and should never waiver from your path. Mental determination, mental discipline, mental focus, mental management, and mental distraction— they're good for business!

LIFE IS NOT A FOUR-LETTER WORD

As an artist, I naturally tend to see the similarities between life and art because the disciplines are the same: focus, determination, hard work. Life itself is a blank canvas. It has all of the possibility of reward, and all of the risk of failure; it will be what you are willing to make it. Life with cancer and chemotherapy is also like a blank canvas. *It will be what you decide to make it,* but you must be willing to take risks. You must be willing to create order out of chaos, to put color and texture where otherwise there would be nothing.

You are stronger than you think. Prove it to yourself. Some people tend to hear the word "cancer" and just give up. Cancer is not necessarily a death sentence. Are you guilty of making excuses and using cop-outs? Our present-day society absolves you of any personal responsibility and will spoon-feed you the excuses: "I'm helpless. I can't take care of myself. I don't know any better. I don't have any family. I don't have any friends. I don't have any money. I don't have any interests. I can't do anything." Are you gonna fall for that? Learn to think and act for yourself. While you may be comfortable in the cradle of society, it does nothing for your zest and enthusiasm for life or the all-important "will to live." This is the bottom-line truth: you have to help yourself or no one else can help you.

Yes, you do have cancer, and chemo is a four-letter word. But now, more than ever, you need to decide what you are willing to work for. I challenge you to ask yourself some questions: what do you want, how badly do you want it, and what are you willing to work for? These are the same questions posed at your high school graduation. Now, more than ever, you need serious attitude management, and clearheaded focus. Now, more than ever, you should be setting goals. Take a risk: decide to change your life from a question mark to an exclamation point! With iron-willed determination, choose your path and start making your goals happen. Hey, maybe today your goal is making it to the end of the hall, but vow that tomorrow you'll go even farther. *Believe in the art of the possible.* Don't say, "This is not possible." Ask yourself, "How can I make this work?" Let's face it, you've got a lot of time to do some quality thinking, so think! If you could roll over right now and look at the rails underneath your hospital bed, you would see my initials carved there. So don't tell me I'm crazy. Who knew I would make it this far, or count the achievements in my career that I now enjoy, *while on chemo?* I sure am glad I didn't quit years ago, when I received *another* cancer diagnosis. If I can do it, you can do it!

It's Cancer
Handling the News: As the Patient, As the Friend

The life-altering verdict is in: it's cancer. Terrifying in any form, in any country, in any language. How do you handle the news? How do you keep from jumping off high buildings or diving beneath the nearest train? How do you tell your friends and family? How do you stop your brain from spinning and remain clearheaded, so as to handle the tasks ahead? Or if a friend or family member has just given you the news, how do you respond? What does he need from you? What are the rules?

As the Patient: Just as cancer is individually specific, each person will have his or her own personal way of handling the news. But I do have a few suggestions which have served me well. Remember Survival Step #1—Establish your C.E.O. Clarity, logic, and common sense are your greatest assets right now. To the best of your ability you must keep your head on straight, while everyone around you is losing theirs. You need to be able to hear your doctor's words, make sound decisions, and not panic. This is a good time to start those deep breathing exercises in Step #2. Remember, people in burning buildings or underwater often die because they panicked. Are you comfortable with your doctor? It is imperative that you have utmost confidence in the medical care you are receiving. Get a second, or third, opinion. If you're getting the same answers, at least you know you are headed in the right direction.

Now for the task of advising family and friends, which can be overwhelming. More deep breathing exercises are in order here. Keep your announcements brief and informative: diagnosis and recommended surgery or treatment, which is all you actually know right now. Try to call just three people every day, and when speaking with them, try to stay calm and discuss the news matter-of-factly. There is a method here. The more that you can verbalize in a rational manner, the more you will begin to handle the reality of the situation and remove some of the terror. You really need everyone to stay cool-headed. If you are calm, then maybe they won't fall apart on you, sobbing hysterically, so that you have to be the strong one, comforting them. You will have friends who are hurt that they didn't get the news right away. Establish a phone chain: tell one or two people, who will keep everyone else posted. Give instructions: "I'll be in surgery for a week, and then recuperating for two weeks, and may be unable to receive calls. I'll be in touch when I'm able." If you are unable to handle the phone calls, turn off the phone and let voice mail pick up the messages.

As you recover, begin your methodical therapy again, by each day making a few calls. Your loved ones are worried and want to hear from you, so matter-of-factly give them a progress report, but skip the gory details. Graciously accept the gifts and food offered. Let's face it, you're standing somewhere between desperate need and eternal gratitude. Always send a thank-you note or make a phone call expressing your thanks. And remember, to have a friend, you must be a friend. You will find ways to repay the generosity offered by your friends and family. One day, you'll be taking gifts to their door.

❧

As the Friend: So many people just don't know how to respond when the bad news comes, so they retreat. They're afraid to call, afraid to disturb the patient, afraid they'll do or say the wrong thing. Unless you've received instructions for "no calls," your patient will probably appreciate hearing from you. He needs to stay connected to his friends. If you leave a voice message and don't hear back right away, he may be in the hospital or in treatment and will call when he is able. Hearing your message will let him know you care and will bring him pleasure. You just read the advice I gave the patient, so you already know that the patient needs calm. No screaming, no sobbing, no emotional outbursts, which will bring your fragile patient crumbling into pieces. If it sounds like your patient wants to talk, inquire about the next step in his treatment. Express your love or concern, and if your life is hectic right now, say those well-meaning but useless words, "Let me know if there is anything I can do."

If you know your patient's personal circumstances, offer to pick up the kids after school, take them to soccer practice, or help out with aging parents. If the patient is self-employed, perhaps you can answer the phone at work, open or close the shop, etc. The spouse really has her hands full, so suggest you drive the patient to the doctor. In other words, your patient is so overwhelmed, he doesn't really know what to tell you. And when he does know, he's so worried about "bothering" you, he probably won't call. If the patient does his own housekeeping, sending someone over to do laundry, change the sheets, or tidy up a bit will be immensely appreciated. Maybe she just needs a shampoo. Make some suggestions so she knows your level of commitment. Don't worry that she'll abuse your generosity.

After the patient is home from the hospital, food is always a good idea. It doesn't have to be homemade or fancy. A trip to the grocery store for something simple and basic is always a winner: a rotisserie chicken and bag of salad, or staples such as eggs, bread, cold cuts, soup, and fruit. If possible, suggest your patient make a grocery list for you to fill. Sometimes she will have special dietary needs, so inquire about those. Of course, you'll send a card— nothing too morose, but always write some personal remarks. (Believe it or not, I still have all of the cards sent to me over the last five years of treatment, and sometimes I take a few random ones out and read them. It always makes me smile and gives me a lift.) Maybe you'll send flowers, but please ask the florist not to put anything with a pungent fragrance in the bouquet because patients fresh from surgery or chemotherapy sometimes can't tolerate strong odors.

When the patient is able, ask if you can stop in for a visit, take her to lunch, invite her to dinner or a movie. Whether she knows it or not, she really needs a change of atmosphere for just a little while. If she staunchly refuses, at least you tried and the door is open. Other than food, the gifts I appreciated the most were ones that made me laugh. Books, comedy tapes, movies, or even jokes off the Internet got me through some really difficult days. And chocolate. Lots and lots of chocolate!

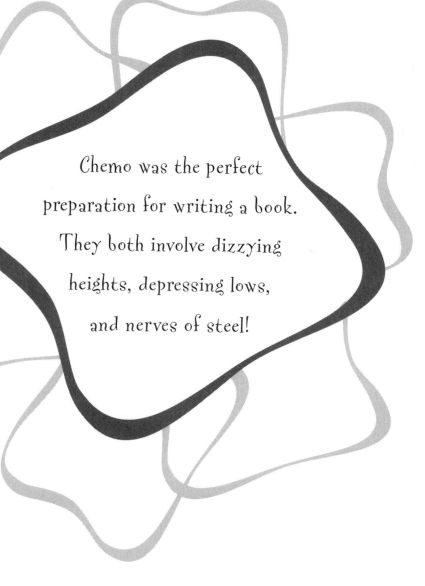

Chemo was the perfect preparation for writing a book. They both involve dizzying heights, depressing lows, and nerves of steel!

With a well-chosen wig, you never
have a bad hair day.

chapter 11

Camouflage Gear and ABPs
(Auxiliary Body Parts)

*C*hemo provides the "scorched earth policy" for the complete nuclear fission experience. I boast railroad tracks, traffic bumps, implantations, extrications, and eradications. I even have a plastic medical port imbedded under the skin in my chest for injecting chemo (it's the Cadillac way to marinate). I'm sure there is enough titanium implanted in my body to make a complete set of golf clubs. I also have beautifully painted, sculptured fingernails (I just felt a need to throw that in). The only things people see when I leave the house are my great wig and those elegant fingernails!

Look, you have a few choices here. You can think of cancer as an organ-by-organ body transfer and feel sorry for yourself, or you can take this experience and make it work for you.

We have all heard about marriages that fail after a debilitating surgery such as a mastectomy. Perhaps those marriages were already doomed, or maybe it was the woman who pulled out, deciding that a brush with mortality was enough to help her realize it was time to cut her losses. But I truly believe that in some instances it is because of the woman's response to her own body. Know this: the world, and your significant other, will follow your lead. If you focus on your mutilated body, so will they. Some people wear their disease and scars like martyrdom—little wonder that they receive a negative response from others!

Let's look at ways to get this body thing in perspective. With apologies to the gents in our group, I have to admit this is where we ladies have some definite advantages. Let's face it, with a carefully chosen wig you never have a bad hair day.

When I first started chemo, I was still a little self-conscious about being out and about in my new wig. One evening when we were dining at a neighborhood restaurant, I excused myself to go to the ladies' room to make sure every hair was still in place. As I returned to my seat, I glanced around the room. *Oh, my gosh! That woman sure could use a new hairdo . . . better yet, a wig,* I thought to myself. *Oh, dear. That poor lady over there doesn't have as much hair as I did even after most of mine had fallen out. Hmm, I thought. This is amazing!* It quickly became clear (in my own, unbiased view, of course) that my hair looked better than that of most other women in the restaurant.

The more times I ventured out, the more often I arrived at the same conclusion. The advantages were obvious. They had probably spent an hour laboring over their hair and it still could use help. I spent three seconds plopping on mine—and it looked great.

Sorry, guys, but the toupees they've come up with so far are not really convincing. On the other hand, thanks again to Hollywood, you guys can "go topless" and it's actually a sex symbol.

Eyelashes? Just stick 'em on. A little Max Factor, the right blush, and some lipstick can make up for a lot of chemo. The one problem I continue to have, however, is the eyebrows. (Yes, even my eyebrows fell out.) I've been putting brow lines on for at least forty-five years. Not only that, but I also call myself a professional portrait artist. I should be able to paint good eyebrows on anybody. The truth is, I can't seem to get my eyebrows on right. They are either flying across my forehead like the Nike swoosh or diving toward my nose like a jack-o'-lantern on fright night. Some days I have what I call the "flat look," in which a straight line seems to be stretched from ear to ear. Every day is a new day in Fran's eyebrow department, where I consider myself fortunate if I'm just able to get them on the same level.

Continuing south, we get to the area of scars and body camouflage. A hearty "thank you" to Eve for eating that apple and creating the need for this whole clothing thing. If it were not for clothing, I'd have been exiled to Saturn a long time ago. My body looks like an atomic bomb test site. No kidding. The cancer started in 1984 with a mastectomy. My lifetime tally so far for visits to the operating room (including for childbirth) is nineteen. I have missing parts, strip-mined parts, and a tangled web of scars that resembles a map of the U.S. interstate highway system. There are dips, gashes, gouges, and even some that look like punctuation marks.

The mastectomy occurred before simultaneous reconstruction was customary. Afterwards, reconstruction was an option I chose not to take. By that point I had experienced a long and painful recovery from the original surgery, followed by months of chemo. I had been looking at ceilings for almost a year. I was ready to get up and out and back to a normal life. Besides, I was more than ready to stop hurting. When I thought about starting all over with reconstructive surgery, I decided that if I had my druthers, I druther not. Why bother? So I could wash two lumps in the shower instead of just one? Everyone has to make the decision that is best for them. I had adjusted to the situation, and my wonderful husband didn't seem to care one way or the other. (I truly do have the world's most patient and understanding spouse!) Together, we chose not to make a big deal out of all this body stuff—so we joke, we laugh, and we have a wonderful sex life. I point to all those scars and tell him if he gets lost, just look for the road maps leading to "Points of Interest." (See, for the same great price, you get the kiss-and-tell version.)

I even make jokes with my husband about the missing part. I never did like to wear a bra and still don't. It rides, it binds, it pinches—and eventually it flies across the room as I free myself from its tortuous encumbrance! As a result, I frequently forget where I left the thing. I could simply reach for another one, except for the fact that the bra I rejected a few hours ago contained my prosthesis, otherwise known as my ABP (Auxiliary Body Part).

I can't tell you how many times I've left my art studio and gotten halfway home only to realize that I'd left my ABP or my hair (or both) and had to go back for them. Frequently, we've left home for dinner or a business meeting and needed to stop by my art studio so I could complete my camouflage gear. My husband keeps suggesting I get a spare part, but it would just be something else to lose. Sometimes when I'm getting dressed in the morning, I'll mutter, "Oops! Is it in my purse? The car? The garage? The airport?" So far I've been lucky. I've never left it at the restaurant, the grocery store, or a friend's house. But my brain is so fried I am sure that someday I'll be putting out an APB for my ABP!

One evening after dinner, I decided to go to the studio to paint and shoved my bra with its ABP in my purse. As I started out the door my husband, feigning jealousy, asked if I was meeting my boyfriend at the studio. "Of course," I replied. "But I'll just tell him that what he wants is over there on the table and to leave me alone so I can paint!"

I want to share a funny story with you. Not long after we were married, my husband told me about a girl he had previously dated. He went to pick her up one evening and, while waiting for her to get dressed, was entertained in the living room by her father. During the conversation, her father was bemoaning the fact that his daughter needed $3,000 worth of dental work and that he was concerned about how he was going to pay for it. He suddenly brightened and added, "I think I'll just wait for her to get married and let her husband pay for it!" My husband never went back for a second date. It's a standing joke in our family that he should have married the girl with the bad teeth. It would have been a cheap investment by comparison!

So what, you ask, is the point I'm trying to make? It is simply this: *hair, breasts, and flawless body do not make a person.*

My self-esteem is firmly in place. I don't feel like less of a woman, less of a person, less intelligent, less sexy, less desirable. In other words, my self-worth is not even remotely connected to that lost breast! The average life-expectancy in my family (thanks to the now-identified, numbered, and coded defective BRCA1 cancer gene) is forty-five. I'm fifty-eight now. So I figured that if I had to donate something to cancer, I'd rather it be a breast than an ear. (Camouflage would be more difficult.)

I am not defined by what I am missing. I am still as smart as I ever was. My friends enjoy my company (or at least they keep inviting me back). I still have an enviable figure. Bottom line? I am still the same person I always was. I still laugh, love, and enjoy life. In spite of all the years of dealing with cancer and the seemingly endless chemo treatments and medical challenges, I truly and completely enjoy life.

I enjoy life because I choose to.

I remember in the movie *Shawshank Redemption* when the unjustly accused prisoner declared, "You either get busy living or get busy dying."

It was not a difficult decision for me. What choice will you make?

Your Personal O.R. Guest Register

Slice and Dice # _____

Date _____

Procedure Performed _____

Surgeon _____

Hospital _____

City, State _____

Anesthesia _____

Technicians and Nurses _____

_____

_____

_____

_____

_____

_____

_____

_____

Your Personal O.R. Guest Register

Slice and Dice #_____

Date _____

Procedure Performed _____

Surgeon _____

Hospital _____

City, State _____

Anesthesia _____

Technicians and Nurses _____

_____

_____

_____

_____

_____

_____

_____

_____

Your Personal O.R. Guest Register

Slice and Dice #_____

Date _____

Procedure Performed _____

Surgeon _____

Hospital _____

City, State _____

Anesthesia _____

Technicians and Nurses _____

_____

_____

_____

_____

_____

_____

_____

_____

_____

Your Personal O.R. Guest Register

Slice and Dice #_____

Date _____

Procedure Performed _____

Surgeon _____

Hospital _____

City, State _____

Anesthesia _____

Technicians and Nurses _____

_____

_____

_____

_____

_____

_____

_____

_____

Fran Di Giacomo

Striving to establish her art career in oil painting, Fran Di Giacomo found herself most excited by the methods and concepts of the Dutch masters. "I focused on seeking out living masters to study with. Perfecting the drama of light, shadow, and mystery has been a constant theme. Fad and fashion will ebb and flow, but classical realism is endless and enduring."

Today her portraiture is renowned, and her still life paintings are in great demand for their lush colors and dramatic lighting. Her fine art originals are represented by galleries in several states, and her artworks have sold millions of prints.

In today's fast-paced world, our senses are constantly assaulted by the noisy, the vulgar, the grotesque, the avant-garde. When you behold a Di Giacomo painting, you return to the world of quiet elegance.